**AUTHOR**

NAUGHTON, B.

**CLASS**

25 JUN   G3

**TITLE**

On the pig's back

# ON THE PIG'S BACK

# ON THE PIG'S BACK

## An Autobiographical Excursion

BILL NAUGHTON

OXFORD UNIVERSITY PRESS
1987

Oxford University Press, Walton Street, Oxford OX2 6DP
Oxford New York Toronto
Delhi Bombay Calcutta Madras Karachi
Petaling Jaya Singapore Hong Kong Tokyo
Nairobi Dar es Salaam Cape Town
Melbourne Auckland
and associated companies in
Beirut Berlin Ibadan Nicosia

Oxford is a trade mark of Oxford University Press

Published in the United States
by Oxford University Press, New York

British Library Cataloguing in Publication Data
Naughton, Bill
On the pig's back:
an autobiographical excursion.
1. Naughton, Bill—Biography 2. Authors,
English—20th century—Biography
I. Title
823.914 PR6027.A92
ISBN 0-19-212257-6

Library of Congress Cataloging in Publication Data
On the pig's back.
1. Naughton, Bill—Biography. 2. Authors, English—
20th century—Biography. 3. Bolton (Greater Manchester)
—Social life and customs. I. Title.
PR6027.A9Z466 1968 828'.91409 [B] 86–16253
ISBN 0-19-212257-6

Set by Katerprint Typesetting Services, Oxford
Printed in Great Britain
at the University Printing House, Oxford
by David Stanford
Printer to the University

# 1

I was resting in the cab of my civil defence van one lunchtime break in the year 1943, parked in a side street near the Elephant and Castle, when I chanced to see a newspaper tucked in the corner behind the seat, picked it up, read a few items of stale news, and found myself at the centre page, on which the *Evening News* had a daily short story. I regarded myself as something of a connoisseur of the short story, having read most of the masters of the art, from Chekhov to O'Connor, not forgetting Hemingway and Saroyan, and newspaper fiction I considered beneath attention. But something prompted me to read that story, and although it was a typical hack tale I persevered to the end. (I tell of the incident in detail, since it was one of the chance happenings which have always proved of significance. Anything I have sensibly planned always comes to naught, but from the intuitive nudge, usually lacking all reason, have come the real changes and events in my life.)

I put the paper down, started up the engine, and thought to myself: 'I could write a far better story than that!' I seemed to have heard that comment fairly often and I added: 'In fact I will—this very evening!' (I had a weakness for talking to myself in those days, but now I find I haven't much to say.) Then I set off on my deliveries to the various Rest Centres, set up for bombed-out Londoners. I kept picturing myself getting back to my furnished room in Lewisham that evening, making tea, bringing out the portable typewriter from the wardrobe, setting it on the table, putting in a sheet of quarto paper and starting off writing. 'I'll show 'em!' I thought. Yet as the afternoon wore on I had to keep buoying up my confidence, since I knew of the gulf existing between the determination to write a story—even when the story seems fixed there in mind and imagination, simply waiting to be written—and the finished work set out in words on paper. I had come across a telling remark of Sickert's about the artist Whistler, of how he had a habit of comparing what others had done with what he was going to do. It seemed that I had a like tendency.

From an early age I had had a fancy for short stories of any kind, and was often on the lookout in comics and magazines for what was then described as a 'complete short story' (novels rarely came my way). I wanted no involvement with serials, which planted a tense situation on the reader's mind and left it there to simmer for a week: I preferred to read and finish, so that I might be free to enjoy the fantasies of my own imagination. Later I had often had an urge to sit down and write a story of my own, but it seemed there was never any paper at the time, or the pen was broken, ink bottle empty, or something of that sort. Just the same, it was a comforting feeling to have—it seemed there might be something behind it. I made a more determined effort, however, when I was in my late twenties. I was married to my first wife Nan; she had worked in the card-room in a cotton mill in our town of Bolton, and had been an outstanding ballroom dancer before we married—far superior to myself, although I had the nickname 'Rudy' after Valentino—and I had done various semi-skilled jobs, weaving and mercerising, and, between pleasant periods of unemployment, labouring and driving jobs. We had two children, girl and boy in the infants' school; then we had our third child, a plump, happy baby we called Sean. I was driving a coal lorry at the time, and for me a bright moment of the day was when I got home, popped my grimed face over the edge of the cot, and got his big smile and gurgle. It happened that our two children got measles, and next our baby Sean became seriously ill with pneumonia. The doctor, a quiet and concerned man, decided that breast-feeding at home outweighed the advantages of hospital care, and as we stayed up nights, using a makeshift steam kettle from rolled-up newspapers to ease his painful breathing, I suddenly realized how vulnerable we were the moment illness struck. I went into a town chemist one Sunday evening to hire an oxygen cylinder, but when I got home our dear child had died whilst I was away.

I write of it briefly and will say no more of that period—I told of it in my first book, and in old age one hasn't the emotional resources to support such memories, and nostalgia needs to be restrained—except to say that it was around that time I found I could no longer amuse myself at weekends, drinking my usual four or five half-pints of beer—any more was no pleasure—playing dominoes or darts with my mates, and chatting and joking. And so I turned once more to reading, as I had done during the earlier married years on the dole, when I used to go down to the public library, borrowing books of poetry, of which I was very fond, also any book of a philosophical nature, any collection of short stories I could find, and Edgar Wallace's *Sanders of the River* and the like—but not his crime stories. I now learnt that it was not possible to take up reading again in the way I had enjoyed it when out of work, since my mind had become unfitted to such recreation. A few years earlier, hungry of imagination, I had been able to take in a line at a glance, and move my eye down the page rapidly, pausing only at the unfamiliar word—'pulchritude' in an O. Henry story was one such, I remember—and although not heedless of all that went on around me, I would refer it to some less involved area of the mind. But I found I had lost the knack of reading swiftly, and often had to grapple with a single sentence to get hold of the meaning, so that what had been a pleasure was now a chore. It was a shock to discover that the mind, like the body, can become unfit if not properly exercised. Any friends I had who read anything at all apart from popular newspapers, were almost invariably left wing, freethinkers, and in the aftermath of the Spanish Civil War likely to be anti-Catholic, so the authors most quoted were Karl Marx and Bernard Shaw, Professor R. H. Tawney and Harold Laski. Very few had read more than commentaries on any one of them, and Marx as a philosopher, with his acute perceptions of the alienation of the industrial worker from his own nature, went largely unappreciated. Solid reading asked for certain reading skills, a vocabulary of sorts, availability of books, and fairly ample reading time—requirements which very few working-class men could satisfy. As I was to discover over the years, the only erudition the self-taught person can hope to enjoy is a wider measure of his own ignorance.

I wanted a bit more than simply reading—there was no author, it seemed, who satisfied a new need in me—so I thought I would write a short story myself. The urge sprang partly from a feeling of helplessness; I thought I might write the grief or disillusion out of myself, and perhaps bring it in some order to tell to others. In addition it would be handy to get the guinea or two which was usually paid for such stories—I wasn't all that interested in just having something published. On that occasion I equipped myself with a twopenny exercise book and pen and ink for the task. (Ball-point pens were unknown at the time, a fountain pen would have been too expensive, and a pencil lacking the serious note I thought fitting to the task. Also, pencils had a smooth surface which tended to slip in a sweaty hand, whereas pens had grooves which made them easier to grip.) It seemed that the moment I sat down at the table in the front kitchen, all scrubbed up and serious, I cast a gloom over the home, and my wife would whisper to the children, 'Sh . . . your dad's writing a story.' And they would look at me in some wonder, as well they might. My mental processes—which were as lively as could be all day, thinking up dodges to make ourselves a few extra shillings on the side, and giving rise to almost ceaseless banter between mates, other workers, driving-pals along the road, and customers—seemed to seize up once I set about directing them: my eyes became heavy, and I would start to nod off to sleep. (I did not understand at the time that though the imagination may be gently nudged into a desired direction, any attempt to drag it out of the corner in which it has been thrust and to force a task on it is bound to fail.) It was a relief to feel the atmosphere switch to normal once I closed the exercise book and stood up. I'm afraid I'm not going to get very far in the writing game at this speed, I decided. If I get but one story written in my lifetime I'll be lucky.

Moreover, I could not escape certain constraints brought about by my upbringing. Ambition of any kind was suspect amongst my boyhood street-corner pals: the thing was, you were what you were, and you left it at that, so that folk knew where they were with you. You didn't welcome anybody who began chopping and changing, or who wanted to improve himself; others were made to feel even worse by such capers. Also, at work the thruster or boss's man was unpopular and avoided—and to me the friendship of my workmates was precious, and had always been so. (Anyone hoping to write a story would have been regarded as odd, not all there.) As for my family and all belonging to me—Irish peasants by birth, now mostly immigrant coal-miners in Lancashire—they did not approve of that sort of carry on, conspicuousness of any kind tending to invite the attentions of puckish fairies or evil spirits. I knew it never did to outshine others, and I recall going home

4

from school one day and remarking that I had come out top of the class in some yearly examination (school, and the ways of school, got little airing in homes such as ours, except for that bane of all Catholic homes, which was the continual burden of raffle tickets to be sold in aid of the church); 'Good on you,' said my mother, then paused: 'But weren't you top last time?' she added. 'I may have been,' I said. 'Then don't you think it would be the decent thing,' she went on, 'if next time you took it a little easier and let one or two of the others come out top—and you came maybe fifth or sixth?'

In addition to having all this against my taking up writing, there was an almost inborn impression of belonging to the ignorant, the poor, and the uneducated—the ones who had nothing to give to the world but the labour of their two hands, and the best thing to do was not to expose yourself to ridicule by writing, but to conceal yourself and your thoughts—keep your mouth shut, stick to your job, and leave writing and the running of the world to your superiors and those in authority above you. So forcibly was this concept thrust upon one that it became a fact of life, against which it seemed pointless to struggle. And I must also admit to a certain idleness of nature, a working-class velleity by which the wish has to serve for the deed. My future as a writer did not appear too promising.

I managed, however, to save up enough to buy the second-hand typewriter, and this gave an impetus, putting a pressure on me to get something down on paper (a moral spur of this kind appears to be needed by most writers). I read of a working-man who had passed an examination by going to bed after work and getting up at midnight and studying, and I decided to try it for writing. It wasn't easy to adapt oneself to the change —there is almost no privacy in working-class life, and any change in routine arouses suspicion—but somehow I managed it, although it went against my natural inclinations to get up out of the warm bed just as my wife was getting in around half-past eleven. But the sense of vocation appealed to me, and maybe I was slowly getting a glimmering of the need to disregard all apparently unfavourable circumstances—'Bear thy cross cheerfully, and one day it will bear thee,'—such as ignorance, awkwardness, and even a degree of illiteracy, since what appeared to count most in the task of writing was the nursing and resolving of some need, impulse or passion. Success of a worldly kind, I was to learn later, is quickly over and forgotten, failure leaving a deeper impression; the ultimate reward being the satisfaction of the work itself.

Once out of bed and downstairs, I rather enjoyed the soothing silence of the night as I prepared for the ritual of writing. First, before scrubbing up, I poured warm olive oil on my palms, added a little sugar, then rubbed and kneaded my hands to coax out the embedded coal dust, after which I would wash and scrub them carefully—to avoid the smudges that sweaty hands usually caused. It was a refreshing, priestlike start, after which I would brew a pot of tea and attempt to get my mind working. Striving to take up reading once more had been difficult, but writing something totally new was far more taxing, since it meant going down to a deeper layer of thought and *work-ing*—and it seemed I wasn't cut out for work. It was like starting up some heavy old engine which had been lying around unused for months, and so unrelated were the labours of the day to the delicate operation of writing, of isolating the image from the miscellaneous impressions attached to it, and transforming it into the right words—which were reluctant to show up—that it seemed perverse to expect both functions from the one human being. (I could go into more comprehensive detail—a temptation I try to avoid—yet I must confess that as I write these lines, it is not the apprentice writer with whom I identify, but the driver and coalbagger who had to 'swink and sweat'.) The sight of the rows of little lettered keys on the typewriter tended to make me dizzy or at times faintly sick. Just as I enjoyed the familiar feel of the big coal shovel—we always called it a 'spade' —so I disliked the sight of those keys. The tension eased once I worked up determination enough to strike them and make words appear. Yet when I tried to keep it up for a few minutes I would feel a nervous constriction at the heart, with clammy underarm sweat oozing out and rolling in cold drops down my side. If only someone could invent a machine which would type out stories exactly as you imagined them! I often thought, thank God none of my mates can see me.

And yet there was the odd occasion when I might get a sentence to match up almost perfectly with what I felt, and this simple act gave me a glow of satisfaction, even a touch of self-esteem. At times I'd be so overcome by the reconciliation I might achieve between imagination and writing, that I would feel a need to sneak out to the front door, sit on the doorstep, breathe in the sweet, cool air, gaze up at the night sky, and try to think of eternity, the soul, beauty, and images remote from lorries, spades and coal. It was as though *something* was urging me on in what appeared even to me to be a vain and hopeless quest. It could not be ambition, for who from my common labourer's background could want more than to have a regular and assured job as a lorry driver for the Bolton Co-operative Society, with a fair wage as far as wages went, and a little pension when I retired at sixty-five.

(If my guiding guardian angel—the one who constantly prompts me along the way—had perched lightly on me left shoulder and whispered, 'Don't lose heart, son—in a few years' time they'll be offering you jobs on national newspapers, magazines will be writing to you for short stories—and those stories will be in school-books forty years and more from now. You'll have films and plays running together in the West End . . . Films . . . plays . . .' 'But I've never seen a play in my life, never been in a theatre in Bolton—let alone the West End. I've never given the theatre a thought.' 'You will! You'll be given prizes —best play of the year—best film script—they'll ask you to appear in *Who's Who*.' 'Who—me!—a lorry driver-cum-coalbag-ger—what would I be doing in *Who's Who*?' 'Disfiguring it—so keep out. Dodge all such publicity. Stick to your own people— in work and in spirit.' 'Come off it!' I should have retorted.)

In the working-class life of that day, as I have indicated, few things could remain private or unsuspected for long, since most people had insufficient mental cud to satisfy their lively minds, and they became hungry for gossip, so that my possession of a typewriter and the midnight writing capers became known among my workmates. It was not a subject likely to generate interesting chat, and nobody made any remarks to me except an old coalbagger known as Honest Tom—he would never make a shilling on the side, and even refused Christmas tips from the customers. One day as I was standing beside my coal lorry, wiping away the sweat which was rolling down my forehead after we had filled seventy bags of coal in half an hour, along came Tom. He was a man for whose opinions I had respect, and we exchanged a few words, during which he remarked that he'd heard I was trying my hand at writing, and I had to agree it was

7

so. 'I'm sorry to have to tell thee, Billy,' he said, in his strong and convincing Lancashire voice, 'that tha'll never make a writer as long as tha has a hole in thy arse.' Tom was not a man to use such language except where necessary, and he paused to allow his words to sink in. 'I'm afraid tha'rt like us all,' he went on, 'tha's never been eddicated to it or to usin' thy mind. That's where they have the workin' man beat. There's no harm in having a try, I suppose, but I understand that them as has had a university eddication have a job to master the art of writing. If I were thee, lad, I'd keep to coal, an' the internal combustion engine.' And with that he flung his big coal shovel over his shoulder and clumped off in his size 12 clogs down the sidings.

Although I have managed to make a fairly good living from writing for most of the forty years since, I find that at the age of seventy-five, I'm inclined to ponder over whether Tom may not have been right. The only hope seems to be that a haemorrhoidal complaint from which I suffer may in time free me from the anal proviso he made.

# 2

How did I come to be living alone in a furnished room in South London instead of my Bolton home with wife and children? The improbable change came about from having paused over an official form in 1939 and then written down two words. They appeared to have but hollow significance at the time, yet had one part of me not forced an unwilling other part to write them, it is possible that I would have gone on driving a lorry and carrying bags of coal to the age of sixty-five. The outbreak of the Second World War in 1939 did not appear to portend any drastic change for us. Life became more burdensome—perhaps grimmer than it need have been, since we were a feckless pair and rationing caught us with empty cupboards—but if you have never been used to luxuries you have less to miss when you are rationed. It was irksome enough, but I remember it more as a nuisance—the constant messing around with ration cards and the endless talk about food. The under-the-counter dodge of any kind I had an instinctive distaste toward ('he who seeks privileges that are private forfeits those that are common'). I had always felt myself to be one of the ordinary respectable people (nobody belonging to us had ever been in trouble or brought disgrace on the family), one of those with less rather than more, as distinct from the poor. This had bred a sense of identity and belonging which I would not have felt worth losing for a black market pound of butter or pork chop—not that I would have refused either if offered me. What I disliked most was the host of petty officials that sprang up, especially one air-raid warden who would hammer on our front door at night when I was trying to finish my short story and yell at me that we were offending blackout regulations by showing a speck of light—one that I could never see—until finally I began to write in the kitchen, for of course no one bothered about back-kitchen lights.

I was a heavy-goods driver, and as such was in a reserved occupation, exempt from military service. I had to register, and recall doing so on a Saturday afternoon after work. The large office was fairly crowded, youths laughing and chatting, the bright ones helping the less so with their forms. I paused at this one question which asked had the respondent any conscientious objection to war. It was an academic matter so far as I was concerned, and truth to tell I was vaguely inclined to ignore it. I had never been a member of any political party or joined any peace group—a mistake, I discovered, to stand aside; had loudly espoused the pacifist cause, but had never met a conscientious objector, just as I had never met a writer. Seeing the word in official print—a peculiar word, and one it seemed which I had never spoken—it did not in any way relate to my feelings about war, and there on paper it smacked of something eccentric or even cowardly. I was, and from the age of seven always had been, of a disposition that sought harmony with others; this being my mother's way as opposed to that of my father. Yet submission I could not stomach: I would not have a mild manner taken for cowardice. (In working-class life this quiet approach allied to spirit will provoke more conflicts than the most pugnacious demeanour, as the occasional black eye, thick lip, and burst nose of mine bore witness, and on one occasion in my teens all three, when I refused to back down to a challenge from a boxer.)

As for conscientious objection itself, I could recall standing near the street-corner at the age of ten, listening to two men talking about the proper way to bayonet a German, how you drove the long sharp bayonet into his stomach, twisted it, and pulled it out by smartly putting the sole of your boot in his stomach, all the time yelling out the obscenities taught at bayonet drill. I took it that they must have known what they were talking about, because on the next point, as to how a bayonet should be cleaned after use, they were both agreed: 'Best thing, once tha can get away from all t'bloody mud, is to look for a nice piece of grassy earth, an' thrust t'bayonet down into the soil, move it up an' down, an' it'll come out clean as a new pin.' As I listened I whispered a Hail Mary and vowed they'd never get me involved in anything of that sort. Yet if I could put bayonets, bombings, and killings out of mind, there was something appealing about the idea of going off to War, perhaps of becoming an airman—certainly nothing to fear at that stage. As I looked about me at the cheerful young faces I felt ashamed of my own finicky attitude, for it seemed I was drawing fine distinctions at the wrong time, when millions were preparing to kill or be killed. Deny it as I might I was drawn to the excitement of war. Yet there was the Sermon on the Mount, the stories of courageous peacemakers, the almost insignificant minority who refused to kill. A quote from Schiller which I had read as a wayside message on a poster outside a Friends' Meeting House had stuck in mind: 'A defeated enemy will rise again, but a reconciled one is truly vanquished.' Yet above all was the feeling that, even allowing for a natural spirit of patriotism in the human heart—and not seeing it as the last refuge of a scoundrel—the thought that I, a free man, made in God's image, would set aside all sensibility, logic and love, and at the behest of mere politicians would go off to maim or kill my fellow man, on whom I had never set eyes or harboured ill-feeling toward —what yesterday would have been murder was today supposed to be my duty—seemed truly incomprehensible. How could any man in his right mind imagine that was the honourable thing to do! I took up the pen, yet again I seemed to pause, then I got a prompting from my Hunch and without hesitation or doubt I wrote down 'Conscientious Objector' on the form and took it to the clerk behind the counter. I felt oddly emotional about it, even though it appeared to be something of an empty gesture. Anyway I had satisfied something within myself. (It was to have apparently disastrous consequences, for within a year our family life would be broken up, the marriage over, our two children in my care, staying in various homes, and myself torn from my cosy home, often living in lodgings in a state of intense unhappiness.)

I did not conceal my pacifist feelings, amongst my workmates or others, yet at no time did anyone disparage either me or my beliefs. It was to prove an odd war in the unpredictable turns it took and the fact that there was more than one switch of enemy: in early 1940, it will be remembered, Germany and the USSR had signed a non-aggression pact, and the allies, Britain and France, were castigating the Russian invasion of Finland, and planning to send troops there to aid the Finns. In June 1940 France capitulated, the Franco–German armistice was signed, and a month later the British Navy was firing on the French Navy, and in July the French broke off diplomatic relations with the British. A year later Germany invaded Russia, the USSR became an ally instead of a potential enemy, and fought a most heroic war.

Not only are Lancastrians tolerant, but they have a weakness for seeing the comic side of everything. I remember when the news of Germany's early victories came through on the wireless we were having our midday meal in the cookhouse, and at once a driver got up to demonstrate how we must all learn to carry sacks of coal with a goosestep, whilst another gave a vivid impression of Hitler ranting away, and everybody laughed. Then one day in the spring of 1940 the transport boss, Tommy, a good friend of mine, took me to one side: 'Last night the management committee passed a resolution that all conscientious objectors be suspended during the period of the war,' he confided to me. 'So will you withdraw your own objection? It'll make no difference to you, since you can't go in any case.' He couldn't understand why I should flatly refuse to do so, but having made my declaration nothing would have induced me to withdraw it (I believe I would have faced a firing squad rather than do so). Tommy had been a pilot in the 1914 War, and as such had every sympathy for my stand, but as he pointed out to me, 'There has always been war— and there'll always be war. You'll never stop it.' I agreed this was so: 'There's always been robbery, rape and murder, and you'll never stop them,' I said, 'but it doesn't mean you have to join in.'

A week later, at a firm at which I had achieved an unprecedented promotion over the years—from temporary or casual carrier-off working under a horse-carter, I had risen to lorry driver—I took my last wages and a handsome reference. 'I have great pleasure in testifying to the ability, honesty and integrity of Wm Naughton . . . In conclusion I have not the slightest hesitation in recommending Mr Naughton for any position where a really smart, efficient and upright person is required. Wishing him every success. F. Horrobin. Transport Manager.' (It so impressed me that I have always kept it, to bring out and read when things look grey on the writing horizon.)

I had a few beers with my old driving mates, who all agreed that it was a bloody shame, and off home I went unemployed once more. And I must admit that in spite of the sorry prospect ahead I felt a sense of relief—somehow I don't seem cut out for jobs as such. Yet it might seem odd that the members of the committee of a co-operative society—a socialist organization of sorts—should go out of their way to dismiss any worker who held pacifist views about war, and that my union, the Transport and General Workers, should have made no objection. Yet it must be understood that the moment war is declared, a decided change takes place in the attitude of those who have acquired authority of any kind, and they eagerly attempt to demonstrate their own patriotism by embracing mass opinion and sniping at those out of line and vulnerable.

# 3

Having taken up pacifism I felt the need to be logical in my principles, so that I refused to accept what would be considered war work. I felt I might as well be fighting as that. So I had to search round for work devoted to peaceful ends, such as farm work or the like. There was no such job to be found around Bolton, and after a week or two I got in touch with the Peace Pledge Union in London, and gathered that the thing to do was to make my way there and then take up one of the jobs that came in from some pacifist sympathizers. So I packed a tattered suitcase, kissed my wife Nan goodbye, hugged my two children, and set off with about thirty shillings in my pocket —not forgetting to take my typewriter. A driver pal of mine had arranged that another driver would pick me up at Farnworth, a few miles from Bolton, and give me a lift to London. I began to feel an exciting sense of adventure about it all. This early feeling, however, left me after waiting and watching every lorry for three hours in a fairly prominent position by the busy spot which had been arranged. It was approaching ten o'clock in the evening, and I was at a loss what to do. I could hardly go back home, I felt, after the tears on my departure. Finally, when I had almost given up hope, my man drew up beside me in his lorry, and I got inside in the mate's seat. He explained that the shunter—the daytime driver who delivered the load which had come up from London the night before—had been delayed. The din inside the cab, together with the vibration, was such that talk could be heard only with difficulty, so that mostly we remained silent; also, the wartime lighting with headlights masked made driving difficult. Nor did my driver, Jim, who was not a young man, appear to have good eyesight. At one time I spotted a pair of cyclists ahead of us, a young man and woman, and it seemed to me that Jim was driving straight at them. They were about two hundred yards ahead, and Jim was making no move to draw to one side. It was a most difficult situation, since I felt I couldn't go into a driver's cab and tell him to watch the road better, yet I certainly couldn't sit there and take a chance. Finally, as we drew nearer, and there was no reaction from Jim or movement of the wheel, I turned to him, 'Jim!' I called, '—cyclists!' He suddenly sprang to life, as though he had been dozing, and with a sharp turn of the steering-wheel just got round them. Being at the nearside, I was able to see the alarm on their faces as they looked up and the lorry sped by with inches to spare.

The old Roman road, Watling Street, was the A5 route to London, and an incredibly strange and often squalid world, once darkness came down, and the night life of the roads took over. There were various cafés for trunk drivers along the way, most of them serving greasy egg and chips with strong tea, but a driver had to keep an eye on his wagon whilst eating, for there was much rifling of cabs: there were the regular prostitutes along the route, a number of vagrant women, and others with a sort of nomadic streak, who liked the darkness and keeping on the move. A girl standing by the side of the road gave a wave and Jim drew to a halt to give her a lift. She came into the cab, and had to sit on the warm bonnet, between him and me. She was about nineteen, pleasant and smiling, unwashed, as though she had been on the roads for days, and the unfortunate girl had a sickening body stench.

I was astonished that Jim did not appear to notice the smell, but chatted her up any time it was quiet, when he was coasting downhill and out of gear. We learnt that she was making for Sammy's place about fifty miles down the road, and Jim promised her he would drop her there. It was a difficult hour for me, huddled in the corner, trying to be sociable, and taking every breath with extreme care. Finally we reached Sammy's with dawn having come up, and Jim drew off the road, and I got out to let the girl get down. Then he came round to see her off, and I noticed he must have taken money out of his pocket, for he pressed some coins into her hand, and wished her good luck in a loud and breezy manner. He's a decent chap, I thought, but an odd sort of bloke that he didn't notice the smell. As I stretched my legs and took deep gulps of the cool, fresh air, Jim went round the wagon kicking the tyres to test them. I heard a retching sound and I looked round the far side of the wagon. Jim was holding on to a loading rope, his face pale and sweating as he puked. I turned away, and got into the cab. Minutes later when he got in he was wiping his face: 'That poor kid,' he said, 'terrible, weren't it? I only just held out.' I felt very small there beside him for the rest of the journey into London.

Jim dropped me off at his depot at Watford High Street around seven o'clock in the morning. I imagined I was in London, and that a few minutes on the Underground would have me at the centre. It took me hours. 'Why, it's even further than to Manchester from Bolton,' I kept thinking, 'it takes a lot longer to get into London than to go to Blackpool.' I made for Victoria Station, which was the one place I knew from a previous visit to London, but when I staggered out of there I could scarcely believe the crowds that were being disgorged, and the rapid walk, like some army marching, rather scared me, so that I escaped down Vauxhall Bridge with my suitcase and typewriter. I had scarcely eaten and felt in need of food, nor had I slept and I now felt tired and weary, and was aware of an intense constipated feeling. I looked round at the cool-faced Londoners about me, heard the strange accents, and thought of the warm Lancashire faces I had left behind, of the voices I loved, and of my old workmates, and I greatly longed to be back with them, with the coalbagger's leather gear on my back, humping the sacks of coal, with a cheery word and joke here and there. Then I thought of my own home, all my things just where I was used to them, of my wife Nan, and of my two lovely children, Marie and Larry. I was glad they couldn't see me now, and wondered would they be thinking of me as lovingly as I was thinking of them. I asked my Hunch why had it hinted I should write those two words on the registration form, to transport me from what now seemed the most happy and ideal way of life a man could wish for, to being a lost soul here in London, my heart sobbing its ceaseless, silent tears for myself and for the company of the ones I loved—and when would the final demonstration be made of the rightness of the move. I stopped at a newsagent's window and read a list of cards offering furnished rooms, settled on the one which had the kind of handwriting I thought sympathetic, and went off to Vincent Square, ringing the doorbell, which was answered by a nice, friendly woman. I was shown a pleasant room on the ground floor, paid my twelve-and-sixpence for a week's rent in advance—although she said I had no need to—closed the door after her, forced back a sob and told myself I'd have to work up more courage. Then I went to the toilet, and felt much better, almost ready to tackle London.

# 4

Compared to Bolton, London appeared an awful place to live in. There seemed to be no proper order, no regularity of life, no mill buzzers signalling folk to get to work, no quiet periods: everyone seemed to be mindlessly on the go, or on holiday. Nobody seemed to be doing anything—to be working or that sort of thing. But I enjoyed listening to the speakers at Marble Arch, and I very much appreciated Hyde Park, St James's Park, and a sort of freedom of speech which was not exercised in Bolton. Perhaps the one place I was most thankful for in the London of that time was the Lyons teashop. These cafés were dotted all about London, and with their white and gold fronts, spotless tables and pleasant waitresses, 'Nippies', helped to make life less unhappy. Many Londoners were evacuated, so that the cafés were fairly quiet, and food was plentiful enough compared with Bolton. For sixpence one could have a pot of tea served at the table, with roll and butter, and a copper change. Few things I enjoyed more than a pot of Lyons delicious tea—hot water was served with it—and a fresh roll and butter. I almost lived on that diet and it suited me well. Often I suffered headaches from hunger, but a pot of Lyons tea never failed to rid me of one. I had been a fairly tough and lean ten-and-a-half stone as a coalbagger driver, but in a few months I lost a stone. I was on the dole, but sent half of it back home to Nan. Later she began work and used to send money back to me.

The other haven I found was in the Catholic Church—and these churches, too, I found hidden in side-streets all around London. There was Westminster Cathedral, of course, to which I went for sung Mass almost daily, but again, there were these small churches, tucked away. I had never known the solitary life before, and had always imagined myself to be suffering from the opposite, but now to get into my lonely bed at night, wake up in silence, to dress and go out, and perhaps not exchange a word with anyone all day—this, for me, the most compulsive of talkers and listeners, was almost too much. It seemed that nothing eased my loneliness so much as to slip into some empty church, genuflect, kneel, and gaze for a moment at the comforting red glow of the companion-light, and then close my eyes and feel for the Holy Spirit beside me. This orientation of one's spirit was never to God in the sense of a human awareness of Him, for, as St Augustine tells us, 'All we know of God is that He is unknowable'; and to say one loved God would be like saying a fish loves water, or a bird air: prayers as such tend to get in the way. It is simply a total turning of heart and mind to the Unknown, so as to become God-guided. All mundane preoccupations lift when there is a moment of fusion, and at once the soul possesses faith, hope, and charity, and one can face anything.

I was summoned to appear before a tribunal set up to judge conscientious objectors. I had no qualms whatsoever, as I was in a reserved occupation, and there could be no point in my putting forward such an objection if it were not true, since I would not be asked to join up. My sincerity, I was convinced, would speak for itself. It turned out that I was mistaken. I made a fairly brief statement to the three men, who were set up in what appeared to be a magistrates' court, and was then questioned. When I began to reply the chairman interrupted me: 'Where did you pick up that word "background"?' he asked. I was set back. 'I'm sorry,' I said, 'but I don't understand.' 'That word "background",' he said, 'is not one a lorry driver would use. I'm asking you, where did you pick it up? You must have picked it up somewhere.' He was right, of course; I had. Yet I couldn't help feeling hurt— that they should deny one the right to use the English language. When I stated that I had never taken a gas mask, he called out: 'You silly ass!' (which became a newspaper headline). My claim to be a genuine conscientious objector was dismissed, and much as I had naively cherished a notion of British justice, I realized that it depends almost entirely on the persons meting it out. From the contempt and hostility I experienced from two members of the Tribunal—one had a most sympathetic manner—it became clear that working-class conscientious objectors had to be dealt with severely. (Fortunately, a letter from my wife to the Appeal Tribunal modified the decision; whilst not accepting that I was wholly genuine and worthy of total exemption, they ordered me to take up agricultural work or civil defence.)

When I thought over the behaviour of the triumvirate—and I had abundant time for thought in those days—I recalled another tribunal of the early 1930s. I was married at the time, our two children were infants (Larry a babe in arms) and although I could get a few days of casual work as a coalbagger in the winter, I was mostly unemployed during the summer. I was drawing a weekly sum of twenty–seven shillings and three-pence to support us all (fifteen shillings and threepence for myself, eight shillings for my wife, and two shillings for each child—the previous amount having been cut by ten per cent in 1930). This sum had to buy all our food, pay the rent, buy the children's clothes, pay the weekly instalments on furniture, and the numerous small extras—and no matter what anyone hears about money going further in those days, I think it may be said that we did not riot in opulence on it. The government had brought in the Means Test, and this measure was interpreted in a harsh manner by the various tribunals enforcing it in Bolton. Not only were the savings, down to a single pound, of any unemployed person taken into account and his or her unemployment insurance benefit either cut or stopped in lieu of this—a practice that hit the thrifty spinner severely and unfairly —but visits were made to each home by an official, questions were asked of neighbours, and an inspection of furniture and all property was made. Anyone owning disposable articles such as a gold watch, motor-cycle, or anything that could be sold was told to sell it, the amount received to serve in place of benefit. The income of every member of the family was taken into account, and deductions in the benefit of those who were unemployed made accordingly. This resulted in the break up of many families, for unemployed sons or daughters left home so as to ensure being entitled to their benefit, and so did fathers of families, men in their fifties or early sixties—many moved backwards and forwards between home and lodgings—and young workers went living elsewhere so that the father could apply for the full allowance. Indescribable domestic misery, faction and chaos were created in thousands of what had been relatively happy homes. (How a ruling class can enforce such wanton injustice upon its working populace and within a decade get them into uniform to defend their country is one of the para-doxes of democracy.)

We had rooms in the home of my wife's sister, for which we

paid eight shillings a week, and as I owned nothing and earned nothing at the time I felt quite secure after the six-month period of unemployment when I had to face my own tribunal of worthy Boltonians, to determine whether they could find reason to reduce my weekly sum. I was a little disconcerted at the start when the chairman, the owner of a well-known and prosperous pork-butcher's shop in town, adopted a hectoring manner, as though trying me on some criminal charge—he was a JP—but another member, a Protestant clergyman, offset this by his warmly sympathetic tone. I was asked various questions about whether I had any money on one side or in the post office savings bank, and did I own anything, had I a motorbike, a watch or anything that could be sold, and which money would help to keep us for a period during which the unemployment pay would be stopped. I was asked about where we lived, and I explained that it was at number 11 Ainscough Street, that we rented two back rooms in the house, shared a kitchen, and that the tenant was a Mr Carr, the husband of a sister of my wife. I explained that he worked for a property repairer, and the eight shillings a week which we paid him helped him pay the higher rent demanded from the landlord for a house larger than the usual small cottage. I answered openly and clearly, even to informing them of the in-law relationship. They turned away and conferred in whispers, the clergyman apparently speaking up for me, as I gathered, but the judgement the chairman delivered was that in their civil judicial authority they had reached the conclusion—it was couched in these terms—that the said brother-in-law of my wife should reduce our rent by four shillings per week. 'You're living with your wife's sister's husband,' was how he put it (he was a fat, red-faced man, and often I had been tantalized by the windowful of handsome pork pies displayed at his shop, but it was an expensive shop and I had never been able to afford one), 'and since he is in work as a property repairer, and considering the state of the economy, and the plight of the country generally, we consider it's only right and proper that he do his share to get us back on our feet by reducing your rent. We therefore make an order that your weekly unemployment pay be reduced by the said four shillings from this date on.' I was so taken aback by the decision, and humiliated by the ordeal, that I could only mumble a few mild words of protest. What perhaps unsettled me even more was the commiserating look of the clergyman, the way he shook his head, letting me see that he was against the decision but that it was a majority verdict. I felt at that moment that his sympathetic bearing did more for ecumenical understanding than a thousand sermons. I could almost have apostasized on the spot.

I went out into the sunny street in a daze, resolving I would keep the judgement to myself, since I wanted no pity. But I chanced to meet a rough cheerful character called Eckersley, who was going in to be interviewed. He stopped, we chatted, and he spotted my lack of sparkle: 'I'm gooin' in to see 'um—the three bloody wise men. Has tha been in?' I nodded. 'Nay,' he said, 'tha's never gone in before them bloody tribunal sods dressed up like that!' he exclaimed. I nodded, 'Aye, wut about it?' I said. 'Tha bloody foo',' he said; 'I'll bet any bloody money they've docked thy dole.' I didn't like admitting it, but came out with it straight and told him they had. 'No bloody wonder,' he said, 'gooin' to see them buggers wearin' a collar-an'-tie! Wheer wur thy brains! They musta bloody sized thee up at once as one o' the flamin' soft 'uns, one o' them who tak' it lyin' down. What tha shoulda done, mate,' he went on, 'tha shoulda fetched both thy kids wi' thee, an' not fed 'um for a couple o' days, an' 'ad thy own britches arse stickin' out, an' fainted o'er wi' bloody hunger, or created a right bloody row in theer. Tha's got to make a bloody nuisance of thysel' to get anywheer wi' them swine. Look at me—look at me rags—an' I aren't swallowed a bite today—I look like I'm at death's bloody door, don't I. I've got to meet the wife here with our three kids—an' what a bloody sight they'll be when they turn up. Oh, I wish I'd seen thee fust!'

Then I opened my heart and told him what had happened and spoke of the kindly parson and how he had spoken up for me. Eckersley cut in on me: 'Tha never fell for that bloody dodge! Well tha bloody idiot.' 'Wut dodge?' I asked. 'It's all a bloody put-up job,' he explained, 'they fix it all before hand 'ow they'll play it. They try to make it look like fair play, so's not to get thy back up—but they're in one anothers bloody pockets. As the parson's wearin' the dog-collar they get 'im to play it soft—put thee off thy stroke.' The instant he spoke I knew there was some truth in what he said. There had been some understanding, some game played amongst them, for it had almost been like a play. That fact seemed to upset me even more than had their pronouncement.

'I'll tell thee wut it is,' went on Eckersley, 'them bastards, justices of peace, magistrates, judges, an' all the bloody boorj-wazee, are set on one purpose, are born to it, reared to it, 'ave got it in their blood—an' that one purpose is to keep poor buggers like me an' thee in our place. Because that's the only way they can hold on to their place. They don't hate us or owt like that—they just think we're only half human an' that they're doing it for our good. I know, mate, I've bloody worked for 'em—an' I bloody hate them. An' I'll tell thee who art worst of the lot—the bloody clergy.' Eckersley stopped as a loud wailing of children was heard: 'Here's the wife now an' the kids,' he said; 'I'll be off—I'll go in an' show 'em!'

I walked back home in some sort of daze, not feeling a sense of injustice—as might be imagined—but a mortified one of my own unworthiness. They were probably right, I felt, what use am I and my family to any country? And, since my rent could not be reduced, the only thing for it was to find other rooms, hire a handcart, and remove our few belongings, in a couple of journeys. We found ourselves sharing a house with an odious couple, who made life a misery for all of us, but at least they were not related, and I got the four shillings cut restored. My only gesture of revenge on the tribunal has been on occasional visits to Bolton, when I stop at the pork-butcher's window—the business is still flourishing—and with ample money in my pocket I gaze on the magnificent pies with contempt and walk on.

(I feel I should offset that act of authoritarian meanness by one of simple generosity—which occurred some months later when we found a tiny house of our own to rent, a house with a front door but no back door. Friday was dole day, when I was paid the weekly unemployment allowance, but more than once our food supply ran out by Thursday or even Wednesday. I mean, we would have not a potato left, no bread, no butter, no food at all except possibly a few Quaker Oats left in the box. On this certain Thursday, when things were really desperate—we could of course have got food from her parents or mine at a pinch, but hunger was preferable to admitting to such a plight with its consequent loss of face—my wife Nan had taken the two young children out, and by chance had met a one-time mill workmate of hers, out with her boyfriend, a soldier on leave. She returned home in great excitement, the soldier having given the children a shilling for sweets. She ran off to the shop and returned with a large fourpenny loaf, twopennyworth of bacon-bits, a pound of cheap tomatoes a little overripe, a half-pound of sugar—we had some tea—a half-pound of margarine, and a halfpenny bar of chocolate for each child. What a feast that was, fried bacon-bits and tomatoes!—the aroma in a hungry home could not have been improved, and plenty of tea, hot, strong tea with sugar in, and any amount of dip butties. Oh, were we happy! And how we all prayed for that soldier—that he have a happy life in this world and heaven in the next—and more than once in my heart have I thanked him since. I always feel we can never know the happiness that might come from such a simple impulse. That good-hearted man could have no idea of the happiness his generous act brought to our little family, or that it would be recorded a half-century later. Indeed, I find it a lesson to myself.)

# 5

A strange experience in those late evenings of June 1940 when it had grown dark, was to stand beside Victoria Station and watch a German bomber plane up there in the sky, just cruising around in the searchlights, out of range of the guns that could be seen splattering the sky below it. At first, people would gather and watch, but soon they ignored such a sight, and I used to think what a rum war it was, with a German bomber circling about over London, and people not bothering even to look up, as they hurried home from the cinema and the like. Such a sight was never reported in the newspapers, or broadcast, of course, and one got the feeling that neither side wished to make a decisive start and that they might come to some understanding. It was a month later, in July 1940, that the big air raids on London began. Being unsettled and unhappy occupied me in a way that kept fear out, and I hardly ever went to an air-raid shelter except for the company—as may have been the case with many others—and always stayed in my bed at night. (Perhaps it was as well, for some time later a bomb dropped on the local shelter and killed many.)

The Peace Pledge Union sent me to a driving-job in Taunton. To move from my furnished room in London, of which I had become fond, to lodgings in a house in Taunton, in which there were two other workers, was a trial. I grow to love and depend on the familiar, and cannot accustom myself easily to strange rooms, beds, food and smells. (I never feel comfortable anywhere except in my own home—unless I am out in the country or by the sea. And I always instinctively seek out faces and sights which remind me of the familiar. Indeed on a recent occasion when I made my first visit to Switzerland with my present wife, Erna, an Austrian, and we stayed in an hotel from which she pointed out the Jungfrau to me, the one image that kept returning was that of a winter morning in Chequerbent, just outside Bolton, when I saw a huge slag-heap covered with snow. And every time I looked out at the Jungfrau I was no longer in Switzerland but near Bolton, and under the snow I saw coal-dust and clinker. Moreover, the mountains made little impression on me, seeming to block out the view, and I was always listening for the Lancashire accent, oddly rare among the visitors there—unlike in Spain, where in summer that broad and earnest accent takes over.) The job was one of driving a lorry all about the place, picking up various loads. After my seven or more years of coalbagging, every other job I did, from humping potatoes to sacks of flour, was relatively easy. Ordinary work seemed a sort of holiday—but I missed the daily sweat. (Writing, whether stories, plays, or a book of this kind, I regard as a form of occupied retirement, for which to one's surprise there is a payment made.) The only thing that made life bearable in Taunton was a love affair I engaged in.

I had married at nineteen and so never had occasion to realize how much I needed the mere female presence as distinct from sex; until one evening when I was attempting to write a story in the cold bedroom in Taunton, when suddenly I heard the voice and laughter of a young woman downstairs in the back kitchen (the main room of the house, where we all ate and congregated in the evening—if we so desired). I think that perhaps what I missed most over that period of self-banishment from Bolton was that I felt no longer loved. Apart from the odd quarrel, I had been well loved by my wife Nan and our two children—even though at times I might play the heavy father, which was rather expected of a man in those days—and back at the old home my mother and father were always so glad to see me, and there was my sister May and her husband, Bert; they seemed to look forward to a visit, and we laughed and joked a lot. Also I had had all my workmates over the years, laughter and chat daily, and my old dancing-mates, who I would meet now and again —and suddenly from an atmosphere of love and mateyness, I found myself in one where I knew no one, and was totally disregarded and unloved. And I suddenly realized how much I missed laughter—and love. Some part of me seemed to shrivel up when I felt I wasn't loved.

My mind went dead on me, and my hearing strained to gather more of that voice. It seemed so long since I had heard a woman's laughter. I was annoyed at the other voices cutting in and taking up my attention, and my heart quickened when the voice came up once more. I knelt down on the floor, to hear the voice more clearly, and then got up and crouched behind the bedroom door. It was a young woman's voice, one that spoke from feeling rather than thought—the kind I grew up amongst. I was longing to run downstairs and join the group, but as I had chosen to stay upstairs for a few evenings I was ashamed to do so. I don't know who she is or what she's like, I thought, but I'm in love with her. I felt that, by good fortune, I had come upon the most wonderful lodgings in the world. It seemed I was almost happy enough just to listen—and I got a new understanding of a man's need simply to hear a young, female voice. Thinking of that voice, and the woman it came from, engaged all my thought and feeling that night.

I learnt from the landlady that the young woman was called Eileen, an evacuee from London, had a young baby, was married to a hairdresser who was still in London, and who kept promising to come down and visit her, but always made an excuse at the last moment. It had been my custom, when I didn't stay in the bedroom, to go to the reading-room in the public library—opened late to accommodate the many soldiers, few of whom appeared to be readers—and return about nine o'clock, and so now I made plans to meet Eileen as if by chance. Everything went against me, and I spent a few suffocatingly boring evenings in the kitchen listening to the landlord, Old Tappin, repeating his evening dialogue ritual to himself: 'Don't you think you'd feel better for a glass of cider? Well, it's all according—it depends what the missis says. Why don't ee ask her? All right—I will. What say you, Missis?' And so on.

I had to assume a total indifference to Eileen when my heart was longing to know whether or not she had arranged to call. On Saturday they were expecting her, but she didn't call, and it was said that the husband might have come down from London, and that left me racked with jealousy. It transpired that he hadn't, which gave me some relief. Then one evening I returned from the library, and there to my almost embarrassed pleasure was Eileen and her baby. She was a smiling young woman, fresh-skinned and plumpish, open and eager; everything a man could desire. Mrs Tappin invited me to an evening cup of tea, and a little bread and cheese, and over small talk the hour or two went by, the most happy I had enjoyed for a long time. Then, when Eileen was ready to go, Mrs Tappin said to me: 'Why don't you go with her—if you're doing nothing—being that the town is so full of soldiers.' I could have kissed the woman I was so grateful.

I agreed, and off we set into the night, Eileen carrying the baby. After a few yards I said: 'Shall I carry Baby—I'm used to it.' She agreed at once and there was the delicious moment of her handing the child to me. Then we walked slowly through the streets, she suggesting we take the quieter road, although it was the longer one, since there were so many noisy soldiers around. I could hardly believe the happiness I felt, with the protective sense I had toward her and the baby. We chatted—or rather she talked most of the time, for I seemed unable to think clearly. At last we stopped at her door, she put the key in the lock, and somehow we both went silent, as we paused in handing the baby over, her face near mine, and we looked at each other, but neither of us spoke. Her breast was touching the back of my hand, and I longed to lean forward and kiss her and from the look in her eyes and perhaps an expectancy in her manner, it seemed she would have responded. But some warning scratch of conscience held me back: she had a husband in London, a child in her arms, nor was I entirely free. And so I escaped the impulse, and just said, 'Goodnight, Eileen!' and she said, 'Goodnight an' thanks very much,' and slowly drew away from me. I opened the door for her, saw her in, called 'God bless!' and went off.

I strolled back to my lodgings a happy man. In my heart, when life let me, it seemed that I preferred sentimentality to sex; for one thing it lasted much longer, did not spend all feelings at one peak moment but sustained and enriched them, and left not a blurred recollection but a lasting memory. I was never to see Eileen again, never to mention the episode to another soul, but that kiss we had held back was to leave its impression for many a day, and, when I was to become involved in affairs less romantic, was to intrude at the inappropriate occasion.

There was another encounter of a like unresolved nature when, after a spell of driving in Manchester, I got back to London and started civil defence driving. There had been daylight air raids around dockland and down to Greenwich, with vast areas ablaze, which served as targets for night bombers, and one day I had had to drive over to Greenwich with a load of blankets from our area in Lewisham. A bonny young woman with a good figure and smiling manner—I find that I am rarely drawn to sulky women—voicing socialist views, proved an entertaining companion when helping with the unloading. I gathered that she was not married nor had she a regular young man, and this news was as surprising as it was agreeable from one so attractive. I had a feeling she might have taken a fancy to me—especially when she brought tea and biscuits along from the kitchen for us to share—and I dropped a hint that we might meet one evening, perhaps go to the pictures of whatever she fancied. (I have never been promiscuous but prolonged continence, I find, tends to make me priggish.) Oh yes, she'd be glad to—it would make a change to talk to someone with a bit of sense, who took no notice of newspapers, and knew what was happening in the world. Now that we were so chummy I told her of my surprise that she hadn't a boyfriend.

'I've got a funny little temper, see,' she confided to me, 'I won't stand being bossed in any way.' 'I should think not,' I said, 'I'm the same myself. Yes, go on—'. 'Now last Christmas Day,' she went on, 'I got into an argument with my brother in the kitchen when Mum was cookin' the dinner an' I was gettin' things ready for her. He's a proper tease—or at least he was—an' he's a year older than me. Mum had left the carving knife on the table, so I picked it up and warned him to shut up. He looked at me an' said, "I dare you!" Now that's something nob'dy should do with me, dare me, because that's exactly what I'll do.' I felt a nervous little quake in my stomach. 'Did you . . . .?' I asked. 'He was in hospital eighteen weeks,' she said calmly. 'Oh there was a proper to-do about it at the time—the police an' everything, an' lots of questionin'. 'Course Mum said we'd only been larkin' about, an' my brother when he came round played up trumps, said it had all been a bit of fun an' he'd slipped an' that's how it had happened. 'Course they was suspicious, it having gone in so far. Lucky it just missed his heart.'

'Look at the time!' I quickly shut the back of the van. 'I'll have to be off. Now I expect I'll be over with another load either today or tomorrow—an' we'll fix something up. An' thanks very much for the tea an' biscuits.' I hurried into the cab, started up, set off and waved goodbye. I felt as though I had just escaped some terrible disaster. And I need hardly say that I gave that depot and Greenwich a wide berth all through the war.

I had hoped to resist further digression, but feel I must tell of one happening, a chance visit to a bookshop, the result of which was to influence me for the rest of my life. The London County Council, which ran the Rest Centre Service, would not employ me until I had passed a driving test, and so I went out on a big van and passed without any difficulty; and then to work next morning to find that I had been given the job of despatch rider, with a motorcycle and sidecar ready for me. It was a vehicle I had never ridden and did not even know how to start up. I explained this to the supervisor, but did not argue or complain, and said I would see how I got on. (My relative success as a driver had come less from efficiency than maintaining an attitude of reason.) We got the motorbike started, and I set off on it. I managed fairly well along straight roads, but turning a corner with a sidecar proved most tricky; then, driving along the Old Kent Road, I found the sidecar kept mounting the pavement, so I decided to stop, get off, and walk around to see if I could think things out.

There happened to be a secondhand bookshop nearby, and, after looking in the window, I ventured inside. The proprietor had a pale face, squeaky voice, and a working-class manner, which at once made things easier between us than was the case in most bookshops. I said I'd just like to have a look round and he told me I was welcome. I saw a lovely book, the *Anthology of World Poetry*, edited by Mark Van Doren, and recalled how, during my unemployed periods, I had got that volume out of Bolton Central Library so often, constantly renewing it, that I acquired a sense of possession. I used to hurry off to the library in the morning, be the first one there, and have all those quiet and exciting book-packed shelves to myself. Addicted readers amongst my mates were very few, but I had a pal called Harry at the time, a side-piecer in the spinning room, who had a passion for the novels of P. G. Wodehouse, and he told me that often when he went to bed at night, and had no candle to read by, or was without a library book, he would simply lie back in the darkness, close his eyes, and read one of the Jeeves stories. 'I know 'em all so well,' he said, 'that I can see the printed page in front of me, and when I get to the bottom of the page I just turn it over in my mind.' I had become almost as familiar with that anthology, so that I knew exactly where every poem was, and often at bedtime instead of telling my two children a story about my old schoolmate Joe Harrison, I would read them a poem. Handling that book once more brought back a rush of memories, and I should certainly have bought it had it not been seven–and–sixpence, which I did not have at the time.

I began to look round at other books, feeling I ought to buy something, if only for shame's sake, after doing so much reading, and I saw a small book, *Of the Imitation of Christ* by Thomas à Kempis. I had never heard of it, or of the author. It was a new book, one of a series of Nelson Classics, and I opened it and read, *'He that followeth me walketh not in darkness.'* It may have been some after-effect of my struggle with the motorcycle that gave the words some new significance. I went on, vaguely regretting that my Catholic education had not made me more familiar with the Bible; then I read, *'Happy is he whom truth by itself doth teach, not in words and figures that pass away, but as it is in itself.'* I read this over again, as something in me agreed that there must be some greater truth, beyond words and figures, if one could only reach it. I think I might even buy this book —half–a–crown?—perhaps I'll read a bit more first. *'Who hinder and trouble thee more than the unmortified affections of thine own heart?'* That was very true. I went on, leafing my way through, nodding now and again to the affable owner. *'Shut out the whole world and all the throng of sin,'* I read, *'sit thou as it were a sparrow alone upon the house-top and think over thy transgressions in the bitterness of thy soul.'* That did it—I put my hand in my pocket and searched for the two–and–sixpence and gave a tense smile to the man as I handed him the money and put the book in my pocket. It was a momentous decision, far more important than getting married, or having plays and films put on or anything of that sort, for Thomas à Kempis was to be a comfort and guide to me for many years to come. (It was not, I should point out, a sudden awakening of that kind, but a bringing to active life again an impulse which had been stifled for many years—and of which I hope to tell more as we come to that period.)

I will now return to the day in 1943 when I read the story in the *Evening News*. (The experience of learning to write will figure a great deal in the early part of this memoir, after which it will have no place.) I got back to my room in Lewisham that evening with a nice little plot brewing away in my mind. The problem was—could I keep it alive long enough to get it written down? It would be no use if I couldn't, the whole thing would be like a boy, catching a lively stickleback from a pond and putting it in a jar to take home only to find it lifeless when he gets there. A story shape had a way of setting or congealing in the mind and losing its freshness the longer one thought about it. This one was different, of course, in that I had made it up, whereas the other stories I had written were based on real incidents, of a sort that I felt a compulsion to tell, almost as though at confession uttering my sins. I lit the gasfire, brewed some tea, ate bread with it and began to type the story (it was something of a relief after the years of coalbagging not to have to scrub up—a simple wash was enough).

I was astonished at how the words seemed to flow out of my head, my fingers scarcely able to keep up on the typewriter. I found it simpler recounting a totally imaginary happening because I wasn't forced into keeping to the guideline of reality or the discipline of truth. I had always resisted invention, believing that what counts is perception—perhaps glimpsing a basic truth under the surface, rather than tailoring real events to fit an accepted story-shape with a reach-me-down semblance of truth. Often it seemed that one had to write about a happening in detail to spot what it meant and what forces were at work to cause it. (Such philosophizing is in my own tinpot fashion, of course, for I know nothing; and indeed the only knowledge such as myself can obtain can do little more than reveal the depth of ignorance.) Still, although this would be only a hack story, it was very nice to feel it was going the way it was for me. I felt like a man who has been used to digging a heavy clay garden, going down two spits deep, then suddenly coming upon a nice, large patch of sandy soil, into which the spade slips, and he need go only a single spit down. It even made me uneasy to find things going so smoothly, so that I deliberately put off the final page until next morning. (Certain tenants in the house—I learnt a year or two later—had heard my typing and voiced suspicions to our genteel landlady, Mrs Hardy, that I might be a spy tapping out messages; she agreed that she had had her own suspicions, but since I was such a nice young man she felt she could not report me. Apparently when my two children came to stay with me over the Christmas holidays I was exonerated.)

When I had typed a final, perfect copy of the story and settled on the title, I posted it off to the *Evening News*, with stamped envelope enclosed for the return, which I expected in a few weeks' time. A reply came within three days from the fiction editor, accepting the story, for which seven guineas—amounting to about two weeks' wages—would be paid, and asking had I any more. I sent six more stories over the next few weeks, and five were accepted (I made the mistake with the other of making it too real). I was glad of the money earned, for I had need of it, and was also gratified that my assumption that at least I could write hack stories had proved to be true. Moreover, I was relieved to discover that a writer need not take the weight of the world on his shoulders when he sits down to write—although even those stories I would not write from the top of my head, for I had to believe every word as I wrote it. I realized that, by taking myself too seriously with earlier stories, I had inhibited the spontaneity essential to all writing.

Yet such published stories gave me no lasting pleasure, and I shrugged aside any compliments which came my way, feeling rather ashamed of having violated a trust by allowing myself the journalistic liberty of writing such tales, when it seemed there was so much inside me—intimate happenings of life itself—crying out to be written. (Although I hesitate to mention it, hack writing always struck me as a sin against the Holy Spirit—from which source all literature springs.) From the start I felt that what a writer needed most was the impulse to tell the story or incident he had in his heart to tell. Living alone as I was, among relative strangers—although I found that the making of friends came naturally to me—it meant I could not enjoy the pleasure of sharing my thoughts and feelings with friends and so dissipating the need to write them; further, by avoiding the radio and newspapers—my main imaginative recreation being from a few records played on an old wind-up gramaphone—I hoped to starve the imagination from the outside so that it would be hungry enough to turn inside for something to gnaw on. The thing about writing stories, I was slowly discovering, was not the care and sweat one took about the actual writing, although that had its place, but the constant thought that one devoted to a story when walking around, when eating and sleeping—when a writer can actually dream of his characters he is on the right track—and certainly on waking up, which allowed the happenings and feelings to shape up into a story form, one as real as life itself, from which most of mine had their source. The next thing was to get those fresh images, which, though clear as could be, might prove as fragile and elusive as dreams, into words as swiftly as seemed decent; I could never quite escape a sense of purloining, or at least cashing in, when intent on making money out of the imagination.

It seemed to my novice mind that most writers became blind to the interesting reality of their own daily and nightly lives, unheeding of the lives of those they knew closely, and bemused by fictions in the head. It would seem fatuous or perverse—unless in the rare instance of one being a genius—to invent fake happenings with real ones around, or to make up problems for imaginary characters when life seemed beset with actual ones. A touch of disguise here and there, and a changing of names and situations, but little more seemed needed. Apart from the basic fact—of which I could not be unaware—that the only way it seemed they might earn a living was by writing such novels and stories, it could otherwise only be mistaken, if not wanton, to add to the mountains of fiction; authors misguided under the pretext of entertaining, for certainly in no fiction that I read was one given any true idea of how human beings actually lived, and almost every portrayal of working-class life and people that I read was a travesty. No wonder the different classes had such absurd notions of how one another lived. I felt it was my personal obligation to rectify this disparity, so far as possible, and I compromised or made amends for my own ventures by being as exact and as candid as the context allowed—in certain magazines you could go deeper than in newspaper stories—and at the same time keeping a detailed journal. (I should point out that it took about seven years before I grasped the idea of how a journal ought to be written. Weather, money spent, thoughts and feelings and abstractions and generalities should be avoided, as should all attempts to substitute symbols or some code language to denote coition or other sexual episodes often of a seamy or scandalous nature. Should the diarist feel that such are part of a proper and candid account of one's life, or of life itself, they should then be written in objective detail. Incidents and conversations written with Boswellian fidelity make the most lasting and interesting journal material, and dreams always repay writing down. Total honesty is of course essential, but the true diarist will never be tempted to lie or even embroider, since it soon becomes clear that the truth only is of real significance and interest. Moreover, it can be relied upon that posterity will surely discover falsehood.)

Another fact I learnt about any story written purely for the purpose of selling and getting money, was that it was totally useless if it was turned down—as sometimes happened. There it was, a few pages of concocted fiction, something to shame one. But I was always to find that anything written from a need to tell has never been wasted, so to speak. Stories and other pieces of writing I have not even had a remote idea of being of commercial use to me have often proved to be immensely lucrative in the long run—sometimes a dozen years after being written and lying in a drawer. (A book, play, and film of mine, *Alfie*, happened in exactly that way; the head of the BBC Third Programme pressed me for another documentary play, and feeling a need to respond for all that particular department had done of my work, I searched in my old bureau and found all the material ready there for *Alfie*.) But any hack writing I have done—it is little enough surely—I cannot bear to set my eyes upon again. Later I was to realize that this inhibition about writing anything of a pot-boiling nature was far more sound than I could even have known at the time. I began to see that when a writer sets out with the sole intention of earning money, putting aside his intuitive guide for a time, and even promising himself he'll return to it when the emergency is over, he not only impairs that particular intelligence, but tends to cut himself off from the way of life and the people he hopes to tell of. 'Emotion recollected in tranquillity' may oblige the poet, but the novelist or even story-

35

teller had better keep the emotion spontaneously flowing, if at all possible.

When it came to signing my name to these stories, I could not bring myself to write William J. or William John Francis—my correct baptismal name—but settled for the name 'Bill', thinking to reserve the full name for when I could get down to more serious writing. (A dozen years later when advised to get an agent I acquired a distinguished one. The first thing he said was, 'You'll get nowhere with that appellation—you must at least have "William"'. I declined his advice.)


The Rest Centres were in school buildings, and when the main bombing ceased in 1941, a meals service for returning school children was provided. Being a driver, as distinct from the staff, my place was amongst the kitchen workers and cleaners, with whom I occasionally had meals. Mary and Sal, two of the old hop-picking breed of Cockneys, were my usual company at the table, and I would listen eagerly to their chat. I liked to pick them up when they were finishing work in the afternoon, and on my way back to the depot at Lewisham would make a detour and run them home to Downham or Hither Green, open areas in South London in which they had been rehoused on estates during the 1930s. Mary and Sal were old friends, and would talk about their lives and problems to me—particularly when I was running them back home, which would take about half an hour, as if to pay me back in talk. I realized that these women had an urge to chat about fairly intimate matters, but situations which inspired such confidences were fewer on an estate than when they had lived in tenement buildings, and sympathetic listeners such as myself—especially one who was wholly detached from all their associates—seemed rare.

Sal was a widow in her forties, with three grown-up daughters. Londoners of her kind used to marry at about eighteen, and the problem she regularly brought up, and posed with a Cockney dryness for my opinion, was whether or not she should marry Norman, a widower a year or so older than herself, who took her out every Saturday night. A steady man with a regular job at the Arsenal, a man who was quiet and considerate, and seldom spoke a wrong word, he was approved of by the three daughters who said she should marry him—the only fly in the ointment being the memory of her late husband, Archie.

'He was a one was my Archie, how he would fly off—wot a temper that man had! Sometimes, say I was a bit stuck for money, then of a weekend I'd give my reg'lar butcher a miss an' sneak off an' see could I get a nice cheap joint at the open market, where they'd practically be givin' 'em away when it drew toward ten o'clock closin' time. Then I'd dress it up a bit for Sunday dinner, see, hopin' Archie wouldn't spot anythink. I'd watch him outa the corner of my eye, see, as he took the first bite an' started chewin'. Then if he suddenly stopped, I'd got to look out. "Call this a bleedin' roast!" he'd yell out, "call this meat fit to give to a man after his week's work!" Sometimes he'd make a grab at the roast and fling it at me—if I wasn't quick an' got out his way. More'n once he's chased me outa the house an' down the street. Wot a man—an' wot a bleedin' temper. But as for Norman, I can't do no wrong so far as he's concerned. An' my worry is, is it goin' to be a dull life married to Norman, after a woman's had a basinful of Archie?'

Mary was in her fifties, with a worn, sensitive face, dark blue eyes, and a quiet manner. It chanced that, shortly before Christmas, she and Sal were talking about what they had planned for Christmas dinner: 'Well, forty pound of potatoes for a start —I've got them in,' said Mary. 'I've tried managin' on less, but when they all come round, together with the youngsters, I've found I've been short.' To my astonishment I learnt that she had had nineteen children. On one of our chats when Mary and I were alone, she told me that for many years in Bermondsey she had been regarded as a sort of 'Guy's Gamp' (the Guy's Hospital midwife—the name from Dickens's Sarah Gamp).

'Not as I was qualified, o' course, but neighbours who were expectin' would always send round for me, often in the middle of the night.' Mary's face used to light up as she recalled those times: 'I'd these two white pinafores, an' no matter wot happened I always had one there ready ironed an' nicely folded away in the drawer. It allus made a good impression when I arrived an' they saw me put on that starched pinafore. An' I would see to it there was hot water, an' everything was just so for the midwife—knowin' that if she was late they wouldn't panic they could allus rely on me to supervise. 'Course I'd often be nursin' one of my own at the time, an' like as not I'd whisper

37

to my lad Ernie—he might be about twelve when he first came, an' was more understandin' than any of the girls an' would be up in a tick—to come with me so's the baby wouldn't waken the old man. Bein' a docker, an' the work so hard, he couldn't afford losin' any sleep.' (I recall one occasion when I had to go out driving on duty on a certain night, and, passing St Mary's at Dockhead, I looked up and saw silhouetted in the moonlight the crucified figure of Our Lord on the big cross—a most moving sight it was—and it struck me that young Ernie when hurrying along with his mother to a confinement might have seen it. So, when I came to write the story about Mary, which I called *My Old Mum*, I decided to use Ernie as narrator.)

Another time I was running Mary home when she said:"Ere, I'll tell you summink, mate. You'd never guess what I bought myself over the weekend—I'd been savin' up for it, see—an' I went an' paid for it cash down Sat'day mornin'—an' they delivered it Sat'day ahternoon.' 'What was that, Mary?' I asked. 'A bed,' she said, 'a single bed—a bed of my own. Summink I've longed for for years. He ain't never comin' home to me drunk no more. I've had over thirty years of it, but now I'm beddin' alone at last. 'Course he's fumin'—he's got the hump proper. But he daren't lay a hand on me now—not like when the lads was young.'

One day I had been delivering to the Rest Centre in Bermond-sey where Mary and Sal were cleaners, and, as I was about to go off, I saw Sal in a passageway. She had a worried look on her face and she beckoned me: "Ere,' she whispered, 'gimme a hand with Mary, willya.' She opened a door of one of the side-rooms allocated for dormitories and carefully closed it behind us. Nearby a small, hunched figure was lying curled on the floor. 'She's fainted over,' explained Sal. I was shocked at the difference in Mary's appearance, now she seemed so small and shrunken, her normal, chirpy look replaced by a white, wrinkled face, her dentures loose in her mouth. I was alarmed: 'I'll go an' get one of the staff,' I said, 'she looks as though she needs proper attention.' 'Nah, nah,' said Sal, 'she'll never forgive you if you do. Just give me a hand with her on to one of these beds.' I stooped down to lift Mary up and was astonished at how light she was, rather like a small child. We put her on a bed, still unconscious. 'It's not the first time she's gone queer,' explained Sal. 'But she don't want nobody to know—she'd lose her job, see. We're safe in 'ere, they never come in.' I felt Mary's hands; they were cold, calloused, and worn. She didn't look the same woman with all her Cockney perkiness gone. In a minute or so she came round, and stared up at me. Sal grinned at her: 'Yer all right, mate,' she said. 'Bill 'ere gave me a hand.' I could see Mary was a bit put out that I should see her in that state, and she put her hand to her mouth and covered it as she got her dentures into place. 'An' don't bleedin' tell me that tale of it bein' your change,' went on Sal. 'I reckon you had that some time past. 'Ow do you feel, gal?' 'It's that big floor polisher they got,' explained Mary. 'Keep pullin' that backwards an' forwards —it seems to do summink to your inside.' 'I've told you to leave that to me, ain't I,' said Sal. 'Now you just rest you there—I'll finish the polishin', an' in half an hour we'll be off.' 'An' I'll be back to pick you up at the corner,' I said.

There was one more incident with Mary, on a summer evening. It was Saturday and I was on weekend-duty, and as I was driving along I saw Mary waiting at a bus stop. I drew to one side and along she came. 'Come on, Mary,' I said, 'I'll give you a lift home.' She was dressed up, and looking very nice, but smudged around the eyes. 'I just been to the pictures,' she explained. 'A lovely little film, *How Green Was My Valley*. Can you tell I've shed a tear or two?' she wiped her face. 'It wasn't the film—not entirely,' she went on. 'It was when the interval came, see, an' the lights came on. The place was full, an' there they all was, in twos and threes, all chattin' away, sharin' sweets an' one thing an' another, an' I looked round an' in the whole place there wasn't a soul I knew. I said to myself, Here you are, gal, you've brought nineteen of 'em into this world, an' it's Sat'day night, an' you're all alone on your own—not a one you can 'ave a word with or share a sweet with.' She gave a grin, opened her bag, and took out a bag of sweets and offered them: "Ere, you can share one with me.' 'Ta, Mary,' I said, taking a sweet. 'Take another,' she said, and I did. She went on: 'I felt dead ribby, lookin' round the place, them all so happy, an' me all alone. An' I nearly started cryin' to myself—so's I came out.'

I have this feeling about writing a story that you should never force one, and that if you'll only attend in thought, feeling and sympathy on the story and the characters, the whole thing will finally present itself to you. When I had finished *My Old Mum* I decided that it was one I should not be able to sell, but when I sent it to *Argosy* magazine I got a letter from the woman editor asking me to call. She was a most fashionable woman, and when I saw her I could not even imagine her reading such a story. 'What a great pity,' she said to me, 'that you didn't enter this for our short-story competition—I should not have hesitated to give it the first prize. As it is, I shall be proud to publish it.'

What I didn't tell her, and what I kept out of the story (I used the fainting episode as the climax, and recalling how Mary's face suddenly showed up a rash of lines and wrinkles when she was unconscious, I made it that the narrator, Alfie, actually saw his mother lying dead), was that there was a sequel to the Saturday evening incident. When I met Mary during the week she said to me: 'Remember when you dropped me outside the Downham Tavern on Sat'day night?—well as I was passin' I could hear all the talkin' and laughin' goin' on inside an' I thought to myself: Why should I go home alone to an empty house an' that bloke enjoyin' hissel' guzzlin' away in there. So's I walked in, straight into the big bar where all the men are sittin' around, an' I spots him perched up in a corner, all his mates round him, an' I goes straight across to him, "Call yoursel' a husband on a Sat'day night!" I says. An' he says, "Call yoursel' a bleedin' wife!" That hurt me, the way he said it, an' all the children I'd bore him; 'course I knew what he was gettin' at—so's I leant forward, picked up the pint in front of him, an' flung the lot into his kisser. "Call that wet!" I says. He was on his feet an' made for me—but there was some of the lads an' the son-in-laws there an' they had him in a flash—an' he knew he daren't lay a finger on me then or any other time. 'Course they couldn't stop laughin' at him, the way he was all covered with beer an' froth all down his face an' in front of him.' I feel uneasy leaving any bit of truth I've learnt out of a story— if it has actually happened, I believe, you must tell it, since it serves to illumine some greater truth —but somehow I couldn't make that beer flinging incident blend in with the character of Mary and the story I had written. I fancy I may have been too sentimental in those early days—and perhaps I still am.

# 7

I must confess to certain misgivings in that I appear to be emerging from my story as a more decent and perhaps more simple sort than I am, although truth to tell I was naive enough in those days, as anyone from a working-class family in the North is likely to discover when he moves to London. Nor have I been able to tell of a significant relationship in my life which was to develop over those years—not one in which I could be said to be happy or at peace with myself, but which served its good purpose at the time and ultimately, I think I may say, was felicitous to both of us. No matter how much a writer may be prepared to tell of himself—and I would prefer to tell all, since truth lies in detail and I find it is the confession of weakness and fault that endears me to others—I feel it to be inappropriate and an act of discourtesy to write of living persons in a memoir of this kind, and, since I cannot tell all, I believe it is best to say nothing. All I will state is that I cannot recall a friendship in my life in which, on reflection, I haven't received more than I have given.

My memory is so keen with regard to countless incidents —many of them recorded in a journal—that to avoid getting bogged down in what would seem to be anecdotage, I will try to present an overall picture. There was of course the War itself—the constant news of battles fought, ships sunk, towns destroyed and, not only the sinister sight—perhaps heartening to some people—of many squadrons of bombers droning overhead, but also the V1 and V2 raids directed at London. From all this one could not escape, night or day. It was in the air—literally so in the news bulletins—from the moment of rising to that of going to bed, and it was in the dull monotonous food and the inflated concern the procuring of it assumed in people's lives, with queues forming as soon as it was known that some unrationed items, such as fish, onions, dates, or cigarettes were on sale.

What might have worried me was that I had no stable home

for myself or the children, whose care was now my total responsibility—my wife had left the home in Bolton and begun a new life of her own. (She was to marry twice again, and we were to remain the best of friends—and I trust I was able to make good for the lack of money in our early married life—until her death at the age of eighty some forty years later.)

My Hunch—I capitalize an intelligence which was my daily prompter—kept me at my writing when I got back to my room in the evenings. 'Empty me of useless anguish and care,' counselled Thomas à Kempis, and since there was little I could do about the children's future—in time both were to go up to Oxford—and nothing about bombs that might at any moment blow me to bits, I felt that the thing to do was to write. I had come to see that my best ideas visited me during the night, when I had been woken up and was lying awake—then sentences·I had written would come up for inspection and be improved, new developments in stories would reveal themselves, and since all this would be gone by morning, I had got myself a bicycle lamp, with a switch on the top, which I placed on a chair beside my bed, together with an exercise book and pencil, and during the night I would often switch the lamp on and off a half-dozen times. (I was unaware of any sense of dedication—it was just that something was nudging me to put an idea down in writing, or suggesting how a sentence should be improved or a solecism erased, and all I felt was that it was my duty to get it right, in the same way a mother might attend on a restive child. And, like virtue, the satisfaction it brought seemed to be its own reward.)

The BBC used to broadcast a story every Wednesday evening after the Ten o'clock News, and I decided to send them one of mine. The producer replied, saying that he liked the story and would I telephone to arrange when I could go and see him. He was a friendly man, a writer himself, and as we sat down to chat he pointed to a pile of manuscripts standing almost knee-high: 'This month's submitted stories,' he remarked, 'and yours is the only one I can use.' It didn't make me feel too happy, since my natural tendency is to identify with failure—a mother's training perhaps, or possibly a Catholic one—and it seemed that they, the losers, were in their hundreds and I the only winner. Then he asked me to go along to a studio to try me out for reading my story, but I explained that it was a Cockney story and I'd be no use. 'Let's try,' he suggested. 'I'd like to get the timing right anyway. You get fifteen guineas for the story—a guinea a minute—but if you read it yourself there'll be an extra four guineas. After all, we're not in this writing game for our health.' Although I would not have contradicted him, I felt I was, and that the fifteen or nineteen guineas I would earn, welcome as it was, would hardly keep me, and that I would be driving a lorry for many years to come—with the writing as a bonus and a pleasure.

I read the story to the microphone and we got the timing right. He gave me some tea and agreed that since I was clearly a Northerner it would be as well to get a professional reader. The story would be broadcast—live of course in those days—in about six weeks' time. Two weeks later he got in touch with me again, telling me that he had tried three other readers but that somehow he preferred my telling of it, and asked would I read it. I agreed at once. On the Wednesday evening of the broadcast, in 1944, I caught the train from Lewisham to Charing Cross station, made my way up the Charing Cross Road, turned left along Oxford Street, realized I was early—I had to be at the BBC at 9.45 p.m., to allow a half-hour before the broadcast—so I went into Mooney's Irish House for a drink. It wasn't so much that I am a rather nervous person, but that I felt lost, going to this strange place to read a story that would be broadcast to millions after the Ten o'clock News. It happened that a driver I knew was at the bar. 'Howgo Bill!' he greeted me. 'What're you havin'? Here, what're you doing in town?' I hedged the question for a time, feeling that I couldn't tell a chap who had last seen me unloading sacks of potatoes what had brought me to town. After our second drink I said I'd have to be off, that I was going to the BBC to read a story I had sent them. He didn't think that much of the joke. 'Nah, no kiddin'—where you off, Bill —got a bit of cracker or summink to see?' I felt ashamed of doing it, but since he obviously did not believe me, I took the BBC letter out of my pocket and showed it to him. He was taken aback—and I felt I'd spoiled the evening, for I am most uncomfortable receiving the respect any of my old working mates feel is a writer's due. Then, at Broadcasting House, I had to go to the toilet shortly before the broadcast, and I took the wrong turning on my way back and got lost among all the corridors. The producer found me a minute or so before the broadcast and led me back to the studio, where the announcer was poised ready for the light to come on. The excitement was exactly what I needed, and I gave a good reading of that story. But a few stories that I read over the air in a later period convinced me that I was no broadcaster.

The director of a new publishing firm, The Pilot Press, by chance had heard the broadcast, and he wrote asking me to visit him at his office in Great Russell Street. He was in his thirties, a gentle and kindly man, poet and sociologist, whom I had met years earlier when he was engaged on a social study of working-class life in Bolton for Mass Observation. I was happy to see Charles—we were on the first-name friendship—and his quiet and encouraging manner I found most persuasive, so that the upshot of our meeting was that a contract for a book was later signed. This was on 8 March 1944, and in the contract I agreed to deliver a book, the working title of which was 'Marriage', to the publishers by 1 July 1944. I was handed a cheque for £30 by the publisher, Kalman Lantos, and I recall how I impulsively spat on the palm of my hand, in the Irish peasant manner when clinching the sale of a cow at a fair. This gesture appeared to please him, and the cheque fairly set me up, for it was the largest sum I had ever received in one payment in my life, and the most money I had ever possessed.

Charles had wisely made no stipulation about the subject of the book, neither, indeed, whether it be of fiction or fact, and although around four months seemed time enough, I soon began to feel anxious, especially as I was at my driving job all the time, and also had to find new places for my children to stay, as the first place with pacifist friends in Devon had proved unsuitable. (Somehow I find that in the long run I seem to get along better with ordinary folk than with those of certain moral convictions—no matter how much they may accord with my own.)

When I had written my stories on Londoners, mostly using a first-person narrator, I had always been faithful to the rhythms of Cockney speech—these, by the way, although distinctive, vary considerably by individual and area. It was the same when I wrote Lancashire stories: the dialect, which also enjoys considerable lively variation within a mile or two of an area, came naturally, but I had to communicate to the reader the cadences. (These, incidentally, are forfeited when someone from a somewhat uncultured class becomes 'educated' and, in acquiring a correct speaking voice, must sacrifice spontaneity of utterance, and with it what Carlyle calls 'the rhythm or tune' of speech; watchful of grammar and enunciation, any instinctive euphony deserts him and he is left with a monotony of tone, laborious to himself and tedious to the listener. Speaking as an autodidact myself, I'm afraid I know the impediment only too well; especially when I meet some old coalbagging mate from Bolton, or even a Cockney acquaintance, it takes some minutes for me to slip into a similar accent and usage. The loss to the poet of a vernacular richness and freedom—as William Barnes was keenly aware—is inestimable.)

After toying about with the idea of an autobiographical novel, I decided to write about various periods of my own life: this seemed to me the simplest way, since writing has this in common with dreaming—those experiences which have to be kept to oneself will tend to be evoked by it. Now I had to find the voice that was truly my own, which was not as simple as I had imagined. I had not yet acquired the quiet discipline writing responds to—that of getting down to the task with a subdued enthusiasm first thing every morning, the earlier the better, not later than six o'clock if at all possible, managing to get a few sentences written and, more important, putting mind and imagination on the right course for the day, before the world and its worries get hold of one. What I did have in living alone was an abundance of solitude, which, once I had taught myself to withstand it, created a sense of freedom from the attentions and demands of others—a privilege which no writer should expect to enjoy under the family roof. It is not that when writing one needs seclusion but a sense of being safe from intrusion— even of a psychic sort from a nearby room. The anonymous human presence will often stimulate ideas; I knew a writer who often bought the cheapest London underground railway ticket, boarded an Inner Circle train, found a suitable seat, took out his large hardback notebook, placed it on his knee, and got to work; then he got out at the same station an hour or so later, having completed his morning stint. Should a writer be forced to shut himself off totally from others, he may be keeping out those wisps of imaginative fancy which infuse his thought as he puts down words. I believe that the more of life—both in memory and immediate feeling—one can distil into writing, the richer it will be; the uncouth touch will be understood and overlooked. Anyway, I struggled on as best as I could, often idle and unhappy, and always feeling I could have done much better. But when I make a promise of any kind I cannot bear the humiliation of breaking it—especially so after spitting on the palm—and on the very day agreed I took the finished type-script, made up of thirty–one chapters, about fifty–five thou-sand words, to Charles at the publishers. I handed it to him, making a perhaps unusual request for a first book: 'Please don't publish it,' I said. 'Give me another few months and I'll make a good novel of it. I won't even take the second instalment of the advance.' This was what I took to be a well-bred and honest gesture, since delivery meant a further payment—one of £50. 'Well, shall we just read it first?' he suggested in his gentle way.

Weeks went by, and I heard no word. It must have been worse than I thought, I decided—what a pity! I was ashamed of telephoning my friend Charles, since I preferred not to embar-rass him or cheapen myself. Then, to my surprise, a cheque for £50 came. Shortly after there was one morning when the post-man delivered a fat envelope; I opened it and found a batch of long lengths of printed paper—the galley proofs of my book, sent for corrections. I was stunned at the sight, and far from happy. Every sentence I now read seemed lopsided. Also, I had followed my natural impulse to write from the heart, not the head, and it seemed to me I had perhaps overdone it. It all read too naked and raw. 'Any critic who reads that will certainly set about me,' I thought, 'and I deserve it.' (Writers are almost always mistaken about how critics and other readers will react, for it was the very rawness that made its appeal and in a way a polished piece of writing would have failed.) Charles dissuaded me from overdoing the correcting, for which I was to be thank-ful, since there is always some indefinable loss when an author takes on the task of improving. (At one editorial chat he objected to a phrase I had used, 'the penis of the imagination reaching out', pointing out that the imagination didn't have one; looking back it seems a rum situation, that of a lorry driver trying to tell a poet that it had.)

A few months later I was having my lunch beside another driver called George, who was reading the *Daily Herald* and had it open at the centre page. I kept giving a glance across his arm, and spotting paragraph headings which had a vague familiarity.

I began to feel uneasy: somebody's got there before me, I thought; or they've stolen my ideas. I leant closer to George and began to read snatches of what was a big centre-page article. 'Mr Naughton has the gift of words and a real delight in the craftmanship of writing.' Then I suddenly realized that it was a review of my book, *A Roof Over Your Head*. I could see the words 'humour', 'laughter', and 'poetry'. I felt happy, upset, and embarrassed at the same time. I was relieved that George was ignoring the book review and reading something on the opposite page. Then I spotted the words 'It has a quality of genius.' One of us is mistaken, I was inclined to think, but who was I to disagree with an educated man? Then it seemed I got a lump in my throat, and also felt ashamed of having told the world about my private married life, of poverty, and other difficulties which I had concealed from my closest friends. I found I couldn't read on.

It seemed that that review set going a spate of notices, most of them on similar lines. The one thing that pained me was when they spoke of our street in Bolton as a slum street. We should never have claimed to be posh, but respectable we certainly were, and by our own decent standards we were as far from being a slum street as one could get. Apart from that, however, which made me feel I had brought a certain slur on our neighbourhood, I learnt fairly swiftly to defer my own reservations about the book to the critics' acclaim. This meant that I had to learn to swallow a belief I had that the book could have been a lot better; and after all, it looked like a form of bragging to insist it was not so good when others were using the word 'genius'. Somehow it did not take long to convince myself, so much so that I soon became very touchy and found I couldn't bear to read a word said against it. The most interesting comment on my 'writing career', however, came from an Old Bolton workmate.

I was on a visit to see my mother and father and others, when I suddenly had an urge to go off alone on what had been one of my favourite walks over the moorlands. (The fact was, that when strolling through streets of boyhood and youth I would come upon some spot which would evoke an intense memory, often one of some difficult period, of going to the coal-sidings hoping to earn a shilling or two to buy food and failing, then walking home sad, hungry, and desolate; somehow the emotion aroused began to prove too much for me and I felt a need to get

47

out in the country.) Then, away on the moorland, up near the Scotsman's Stump, I spotted a solitary figure approaching in the distance; at once I felt there was something familiar in the walk, and I recognized Honest Tom. We stopped and chatted warmly, during which he said he envied me being able to go to the Albert Hall and hear the *Messiah*. I remembered how he had told me I should never become a writer—and I had a feeling it was on his mind—but the only comment he made was as we were shaking hands and parting: 'About your writing, Billy,' he said, 'I'd like to wish you luck, and although they say the pen is mightier than the sword, I doubt it's mightier than the spade.' And leaving me there to weigh up his words he went off in the mist.

In my sixties I made it a rule to avoid reading any review or notice of a book or film of mine, and found this had numerous benefits. For a start there was little one could do about any criticism or advice, since the work was finished—I made an exception of stage plays, which one could always improve. Moreover, it seems that a writer will often find a dozen things he wished he had done differently to a critic's one. A flattering notice, I found, tended to please but make me uncomfortable, since I felt an obligation to respond to such, but thought it not quite proper to do so; also, it gave me nothing to feed on. A hostile notice—most rare I must say—usually meant that the critic and myself had little in common. On more than one occasion in this later period I was to find myself in the company of critics who apologized for a severe notice given to a radio or other play of mine, and it was a relief to be able to assure them that they need not worry as I had not read it. A more telling reason, however, is the fact that an author usually writes from a private pocket of feeling, often rashly exposing sensibilities perhaps wiser kept to himself, and in that vulnerable state tends to take criticism to heart instead of to mind. Praise, I find, has a way of disappearing like froth, but harsh criticism seems to leave a smudge on the work itself, and stains the writer's memory like an irritant dye.

*A Roof Over Your Head* went into three impressions during the first four months of publication, totalling around fifteen thousand hardback copies. Charles suggested I write a piece for his sociological magazine *Pilot Papers*, about a London character I had worked alongside and told him stories about. This resulted in an article called 'The Spiv', which was reprinted in the *News*

*Chronicle.* Although the word had been used in two novels of an earlier period it had no currency whatever except among certain near-criminal pockets in London. Indeed, I would challenge anyone to find use of it in any newspaper preceding my 'Spiv' piece (and, I could almost say, so avid was the public need for such a word to describe the various kinds of smart operators which the war and rationing had produced, find any newspaper in which, for a long time after it, it did not appear in one context or another). I was surprised at the time, when listening to a broadcast by that sober Prime Minister, Mr Atlee, to hear him use the word 'spiv'—an expression he could never have heard until 1945.

Then began a flurry of speculation from etymologists and others about the origin of the word. A famous lexicographer, with whom I became acquainted later in the British Museum reading-room where he was a conspicuous figure in the 1950s, explained in an article that there was nothing new about the word—not mentioning that it was absent from his own *Dictionary of Slang* of 1937. It came from 'spiffing' meaning dandified; the adjective 'spiff' becomes a noun, and changes to 'spiv' because that is easier to pronounce—and so on, in the way of etymologists. This fallacy became common opinion, and even a later editor of Fowler was rash enough to accept it, assuming the word to be an invented one, as the editor suggested, of an onomatopoeic nature. I learnt the real origin of the word from a man who was a vagrant around London in the 1920s. In those days, he told me, it was customary for the police from a certain West End police station to keep that area of London free of tramps and beggars. A man of disreputable appearance daring to walk around Belgravia would be taken into custody, and described on the charge–sheet as 'Suspected Person: Itinerant Vagabond', with the capital letters prominent. The word 'spiv' is a simple acronym, and was probably coined by someone in the police station, used only by those acquainted with such types.

Within a week of the *News Chronicle* article appearing, I had magazine editors and others taking me out to meals, and almost pleading with me for articles and stories. The *Daily Express* features editor asked me to go in and see him, and at once offered me a job, which I declined. I felt that I hadn't made the leap from coalbagger-driver to get myself side-tracked into journalism. My old story editor at the *Evening News* asked me to lunch and complained that I hadn't been sending him any stories. I explained that the commissioning of the book had been the reason, and although I felt hesitant about mentioning it, I got myself to say, in a jocular manner so as not to give offence: 'But your paper pays only seven guineas a story, and this magazine has offered me twenty–five guineas for a thousand-word story.' 'But of course we'll pay you that,' he replied at once. On my way home I began to reckon up how much I had been missing by not asking for more.

8

I grew to discover such satisfaction in my writing that I felt I had at last come into an inheritance of sorts, perhaps a little late at thirty-five, but no less welcome. I couldn't believe my good fortune. It seemed to me that the one thing I had needed in 1939 to get me going was a war, and then for me to register as a pacifist, get sacked from my regular driving job—which I had come to look on as one for life—and to live alone for a time in a strange place so that I could train myself to be independent, while, in solitude, slowly learning how to write, and at the same time withstanding the disappointments and buffetings that are an essential part of such a life. It rather confirmed a belief I have that our main paths in life are decided for us by a series of fortuitous happenings, and that all ambition is misconceived—the best thing is to keep faithful to one's true aspiration and accept what comes of it. Often I would think back on my old coalbagging years, and reflect how I would have had to work and sweat for a month to earn less than I got for a story that might take a couple of days to write.

Now that, in May 1945, the war in Europe was over, it needed no resolution on my part to decide to give up driving for good and settle down to live by writing. Although largely I had lived alone over those years, the domestic circumstances of my life were now becoming such that in all propriety, let alone decency, I should have applied for a divorce and married my then partner. But the prospect of taking up again the responsibilities as head of a family, especially one of suburban respectability, was one which some deep feeling in me went against. Middle-class conversation I found lifeless, and got more interest, fun, and above all material for stories from one evening with a Cockney pal than from a year of the other. Moreover, the idea of some needed material success made no appeal to me; by my own measure I was as successful as I wished to be, and resisted the mantle of 'author', regarding myself—as I still do—as a retired coalbagger, on to a good thing with the profitable recreation of writing, and the pleasurable one of reading. I felt I had a lot of time to make up in that area. So, against my better nature, but remaining true to my Hunch—it fails only when I attempt to tell it what to tell me—I resisted marriage. Finally, some time later, the parting at Victoria Station was most amicable and understanding, if somewhat sad. It was to prove to be the best thing—a liberation of sorts all round.

All I wanted now was to see that Marie and Larry were all right, send money home to my mother and father, avoid getting into debt, and get on with what I now took to be my writing mission in life. I had become absorbed in writing a journal, recording in detail the passing scene, and the writing was of such an intimate nature that it could not be published in my lifetime. (I should perhaps add that I soon ran out of cash and rather than do what I took to be hack writing I applied for a job as a loader-and-driver, having my old driving reference handy. The coal merchant showed me the lorry, then took me round the coal-sidings, which I found an oddly nostalgic and moving experience, and just as I had agreed to start next morning, he looked round the sidings at all the men at work, turned to me: 'I don't think a chap like you ought to do a job like this,' he said. 'Why don't you look out for something better?' I willingly agreed to do so, and after seeing once again what hard work was really like I hurried home and quickly got down off my artistic horse, wrote a story or two for the *Evening News*, went to see the *Picture Post* editor, and arranged to do some articles for him, and more stories for *Lilliput*—anything to keep the pot boiling.)

Now to return to the immediate post-war period. A certain memory of the war years clung in my mind, and particularly that of a promise I had made to myself. It had been Easter time, when the children were evacuated, staying at the home of a pacifist friend in Devon, a most concerned young man whom I had met when he was in the Friends Ambulance Unit in London during the 1940 air raids. Hitch-hiking to Devon from London proved difficult, since soldiers were naturally given lifts in preference to civilians: the first night I got stranded in Somerset and slept in a field, an eerie and damp experience. When I arrived at their home in Bovey Tracey, the wife of my friend told me that since the arrangement was made she had had word that her husband was getting an Easter break, so that not only could she not put me up as she had fixed, but she would like me to find a place for my two children also, as she wanted to have the home for herself and husband and their own two children; the best she could suggest would be to take mine down to her daily help in the village and see what she could do. I agreed at once. I disliked being under an obligation to an ungracious person, and set off with the children to the farm labourer's cottage where the daily help lived. She was most sympathetic, distressed in fact, and said she would gladly put us up, but the fact was she had no spare bed. That was no problem, I said, we'd sleep on the floor. She took us in and up to a small bare bedroom. It did seem rather cold and empty, but it was free of tension, and I assured her it would make a welcome change from London. Marie and Larry were glad to get away from their new home and to have me to themselves, and although I put on a cheerful manner that night as we undressed in the bare room, then knelt and said our prayers, exchanged our goodnight kiss, after which I listened to all that they had to tell me, I was in poor shape for sleep. I hadn't eaten a proper meal for days, was constipated, nervous, and short of money, and all the time trying to assume an air of self-assurance. The floor without mattress proved unexpectedly hard, and the blankets—which I felt the couple must have taken from their own bed—lacking in warmth, so that after a time I had to get up and put on my clothes. When the children went off to sleep I lay there for hours in the dark, reflecting that by my so-called conscientious objection to war, I should have been the cause of my two uncomplaining children being deprived of what I now saw had been our secure and cosy home in Bolton. Had I been able on that night to have my choice over again, I would surely have taken the easier way.

Next I found them a place in the country with a kindly and easy-going family, where they were happy, but when they came to me for the summer holiday I could see that both of them were continually itching and scratching, and after a day or two I realized they had scabies. This mite burrows into the skin, and the lesions can be spotted on the webs between the fingers. Eradicating that complaint proved a most trying task under the circumstances. I was well aware that what tribulations I might have to bear were nothing compared with the affliction and suffering of millions, but this reflection brought little comfort. I began to nourish a longing to see old Ireland, and vowed that if ever I got a chance I would go back home to the place of my birth—to County Mayo. ('Mayo is the county where everything pleases, / Of berries and all kinds of fruit there's no lack,' proclaims the blind Raftery, poet and fiddler, himself a Mayo man. 'And could I but stand there in the heart of my people, / Old age would fall from me and youth would come back.') In July 1945 I set off for a taste of Ireland, leaving the two children in safe and tender care.

Rupert Brooke, enthusing in a newspaper article over the graciousness and dignity of the Polynesian people of Samoa, and at some pains to convey his impression of a courtesy he had never before encountered, wrote as follows: 'A man I met in some other islands, who had travelled much all over the world, said to me, "I have found no man, in or out of Europe, with the good manners of the Samoan, with the possible exception of the Irish peasant." ' I, who feel largely at ease in any company—apart from that of boors—became aware, when back among my own people of Mayo, of a sense of being gauche and ignorant when I compared certain of my reactions with those of my peasant relatives. Not only that, but their eloquence, wit, and warmth made me realize what I had been denied by my English industrial upbringing. I recall how my cousin Willie introduced me to a man who shook my hand firmly, but when Willie added, 'Bill is Maria Fleming's son,' the man took my hand again and embraced me. 'I knew your mother well,' he said, 'she was a woman of great feeling—she had nature for every living thing, from God downwards.' The word *nature* has deeper significance to the Irish, meaning an impulse to identify with and love, and to possess it for all 'from God downwards' left nothing out (and I might add that it was almost true—there was but the rare exception).

Peasant protocol, I learnt, was of a singularly sensitive kind. On the morning after my arrival, when I was about to make my first call on the neighbours in the village, I was given details of the order of my visiting by Maria, the mother of my third cousins, Willie and Delia. 'When you go out and down along the little road try would you keep to the left—for although you'll pass one house on your right, the MacNamaras on the left are closer to you, bein' related to both your mother and father, so you will visit them first. When you come out cross to the right an' go back a bit, an' the next house will be there.' And she went on explaining to me the varying degrees of kinship of each family, and how these must be observed so that no suspicion of a slight could be felt by anyone, but it must all be done naturally. (I had given her a copy of my book and I thought she showed herself an astute critic: 'Wouldn't it be a great thing altogether', she said, after reading it, 'if some clever man from a newspaper was to take all them pieces an' put them together to make a book! Shure you'd be made.' Another one was more adulatory: 'Troth an' you'll have Bernard Shaw in the ha'penny place if you can keep that up.')

It was something of an ordeal to visit a half-dozen homes, and eat and drink in each one. I kept the food mainly to soda cake and the drink to tea and whiskey, although boiled chicken had been prepared in two of the homes, of which I took a nibble. Then I had to walk a little way to call on two sisters, Bid and Anne Grourke, one aged eighty-nine and the other ninety-four. It was a bare room with an earthen floor I entered, but the two old ladies dressed in dark clothes could not have been more dignified and gracious had it been a palace. The elder sister told me she remembered me well, that the last time she saw me was in our little shop, when I was four years old, a wet day it was, she said, and my father was going to the fair in Ballyhaunis, and my mother made tea for her—in this manner she brought alive a day over thirty years back as though it had been the day before. Then she prepared to make tea, and I explained: 'Maria said she would put the potatoes on for our meal when she saw me crossing the big hill, and as that was over an hour ago maybe I ought go off now and spare you the trouble.' 'Is it trouble— trouble,' she said in a strong if somewhat shaky voice. 'Now let me tell you that if that table there was loaded with richest an' rarest of food'—and she pointed to the bare wooden table in the middle of the room—'loaded that the four legs of it would be crackin', it would be little enough to give to a son of your mother!' Maybe it was the whiskey that did it, for, although I kept a hold of my feelings in the house, they got the better of me when I left and went walking down the road.

(Such rich sentiments appear to be given a dry balance by the nicknaming of almost every person. I asked my cousin Willie were there any nicknames as in the old days, and he had no difficulty in naming well over a hundred colourful ones, the following being a few from the list I made: Screecher Finn, Ferret Flatley and Wild Goose Flaherty, Grabber Waldron, Cockstick Egan and Redbreast MacDonagh, together with Bullockeen Conboy, Hi–ho Connell and Swinger Coleman, not forgetting Ranther Duffy, Shiner Kilgallow, Reelfoot Connell, Bladder MacHugh, Blackguard Kilkenny, and dozens more.)

'Humanity is just as perfect in the poorest and most despised man as in the Pope or the Emperor,' Eckhart tells us, 'for mankind in itself is dearer to me than the man that I am myself.' I had been brought up to respect the human dignity of a person no matter how apparently low or even depraved life had brought such a one, and to recognize an individual's nature being something he could do precious little about, so that if one had the most violent quarrel with someone who was a blatant liar, it would be unforgivable to call him such. By voicing a person's inherent weakness, such as meanness or drunkenness, you were touching on the source of a possible God-given trait, and heaven knows what wrath you could be drawing on yourself by taking away another's self-esteem. Some substitute defect of which he was guiltless could of course be flung at him. You could call a thief a blackguard, or a mean person a drunk, but you never went too near the bone. Yet I had no idea to what degree such tolerance could be taken in Mayo. For instance, there was a shopkeeper charging almost nine times the legal price for off-the-ration tea, and five times the price for bicycle tyres, which had been allotted him at a controlled price, and on top of this I found he had the effrontery to put extra coppers on the price of a packet of cigarettes—which in all the war years I had never known happen in England. But when I remarked on this to my cousin after he had paid the extra, he seemed surprised at my indignation: 'Och, sure isn't he nothin' but an ould huckster—an' all belongin' him—what else would he do?' It was plain to see that the decent Irish people would gain little from any future period of prosperity.

Callers of one kind or another were frequent (the word 'beggar' was unheard, and would have been considered demeaning; a person mentally handicapped was spoken of as 'innocent'), and the hospitality accorded such was not stinted. A man known as Pat the Basket entered the house one day, placed his basket on the table, and went down on his knees, hands over his eyes, reciting the Rosary. The family joined in of course. 'He keeps his fingers open to see the eggs an' butter that are put into the basket,' Willie told me, 'and he won't let you up off your knees until he thinks it's enough.' He later remarked to Pat: 'The Lord save us, Pat, but you're a great man altogether at the prayers!' 'And why wouldn't I be,' said Pat. 'Isn't it my job!' As Willie said, Pat swapped prayers for eggs. Tinkers and the children of tinkers called, and each one was given something and took a little more—if it was only a sod of turf from the reek (which had to be overlooked). Stories were told of a well-known pair of travellers, Breege O'Shruge and her tall son Mitchell, of how she would be prompting him: 'Keep your eye off the decent woman's cakes—an' you're watchin' now I see for a couple of boiled eggs no less—an' your mug of tea emptied at one go—the divil shoot you.' And since the pair were homeless they often had need of a bed, which would be made on the hearth beside the turf fire. Mitchell went over to work in England, and as neither of them could read or write, no letters were exchanged. Then the mother died, and a neighbour who later came across Mitchell in a lodging-house in Yorkshire was reluctant to break the news. 'Did you hear Mitchell, that your poor mother died?' Mitchell looked up from his food: 'Did she so!' he said. Then after a moment he blessed himself and remarked, 'God rest her soul, but it'll be ease to her poor bones surely.'

Although the Rosary might be said some evenings, and everyone went to Mass on Sunday, the religious ambience was less rigid than that of more sophisticated places. One evening there was much talk of ghosts and the belief in them, when one man spoke out: 'Arra go on—wouldn't a man who believed in ghosts believe in holy water!' Mention was made of a miracle of sorts that had recently happened after a visit to the shrine at Knock. A man from Ballyhaunis had a large, dark growth on his nose, which the doctor told him might mean a trip to a Dublin hospital; the man, egged on by his wife, decided he would make a pilgrimage to the shrine some seven miles away. It was a hot day, and after he had made the Stations of the Cross on his knees all round the fourteen stations in the open air, he felt in poor shape, the growth increasing in size, it seemed, from the hot sunshine, and so he went into the nearby bar and drank a few pints of stout. It was a good walk back home in the dark, and when he got near his own place he took a short cut that

57

ended by his having to climb a stone fence. He recalled standing on top of the fence, his senses reeling somewhat, and the next thing he fell forward on his face. He lay there on the ground for a time, picked himself up, and made for home. When he went in the house his wife let out a cry! 'What's on you, woman?' he asked. 'The thing—the thing on your nose,' she cried, 'the Lord save us but isn't it gone!' He felt at his nose, and looked into the glass, and sure enough the growth had disappeared. The nose was as clean as a whistle. He must have caught it on a sharp stone when he fell. And no sign of it was seen again. And the question was: Could this be regarded as a miracle?

My closest relative, Aunt Ellen, an elder sister of my mother, lived alone nearby in an old stone cottage that had been the family home. She was in her late seventies, a lively and independent woman, something of a character in the village. Although I had of course gone straight to her when I arrived, she had arranged for me to stay with cousins who lived just opposite. I always went across to Aunt Ellen around midday, and spent most evenings with her. 'I was neither married nor let alone,' she told me on one visit, 'for didn't that ould critahaun Thatch Burke get so drunk on the weddin' night that comin' in that door he fell an' split his leg in two. An' when he got out of bed wasn't it near the feast of St John, when the men set off to England to work at the hay. He needed but the single pass money, for that was the last time I ever set sight on him—an' small loss surely.' Thatch was seen occasionally in some pub or lodging-house in England by a neighbour, but he never wrote home or sent a penny, and my aunt brought up the one child of the union, my cousin Mary Kate, who went to America and settled there. Daughters were regarded as a bigger responsibility than sons, since their destiny was usually America—the American Wake the farewell was often called, since few of them ever journeyed home again; one old man nearby would always commiserate with the mother over the birth of a girl: 'God save us, another New Yorker!'

Thatch Burke was only one of a number from the West of Ireland who went off to England never to return, although it was most rare for a married man to go missing. He and others like him would be met occasionally in some pub or lodging-house by a neighbour working at the hay. The fact was, the

'When your mother came back from America—and as I heard her say of the years there, "It was many the night went by before I slept on a dry pillow"—the matchmakers got busy and they had two great ones here at the time,' said my aunt. Matchmaking, I was given to understand, asked for a sort of inspired judgement, for although a corresponding material balance had to be reached between the parties, it was also necessary to match temperaments, since it would be disastrous to marry a quick-tempered man to a woman of a similar spirit, or indeed a lazy man with a strooleen who wouldn't raise a hand. The average match at about the turn of the century would be that of a man around thirty, probably the eldest son who was 'in for the land', as the saying went, the others being scattered abroad in England and America. The prospective bride would be the daughter of a publican or shopkeeper or maybe a Yank, someone who could bring money in to help to buy a cow or a horse. 'A holding of land', a term I heard often as a boy, was usually a smallholding, between five and ten acres of somewhat stony soil, but as its possession — it was actually rented—meant a certain independence, and in famine years often meant the difference between life and death, it was always spoken of as something most precious. (Although I recall one man who was asked about the size of the family land and replied: 'Sure I couldn't rightly say, but I know that when I was workin' over in England I often spaded more land onto a wagon in a mornin' than I and all belongin' me ever had in Ireland.')

In most cases the man and woman would be from different villages, since in their native village it would be hard to find a couple not debarred by consanguinity. Good looks, wit, and intelligence might play a part in getting the match fixed, and a good family name was important, but the main consideration from the man's side was the sum the woman 'brought in' (the word dowry was not used), and of course it was essential that she enjoyed good health, would bear healthy children, and could work about the place when himself had to go over to England to earn money during the hay season. Once the match had been mooted and soundings taken all round, and it was learnt that the sets of parents or near relatives were not wholly against the idea, and the parties to the marriage let it be seen they were not entirely unwilling, the discussions, of a tactful exploratory nature, would begin. The actual details would remain at a tentative stage, as each party was inclined to hint at unreal demands. The big step would be an invitation to the proposed bride's people to visit the home of the would-be-groom, on some Sunday evening—that is around four o'clock. This hour of the day had a sort of non-binding informality about it, and the uncommitted aspect of the affair would be stressed. The young man and his family would have worked hard to prepare for this meeting, whitewashing, repairing fences, and a dozen jobs that might have been neglected for years. They would be the party on trial, so to speak, for the visitors' portion to the proposed match—the woman and the money she brought in—allowed for little camouflage.

The man needed to represent the young woman on such an errand was a capable uncle or elder cousin, preferably one not too close to her, such as father or a brother, but someone who could appear to be detached, and whose praise would sound convincing rather than extravagant; he also had to be a man with a keen eye for sizing up land. There would be a party of maybe three or four—an elder brother might attend but never of course the girl herself—and when they arrived they would be offered tea before they looked round the place, but usually they preferred to wait. The comments of the inspecting party would be no indication to a stranger of their true feelings, although clear enough to the young man's people. If they disapproved of a place and a family—and a wink would be enough amongst themselves—they were inclined to make compliments, although it would not need a sensitive ear to detect a certain irony. With profuse thanks they would refuse tea, explaining that they had someone to meet and were in a great hurry, and would not bring out the bottle of whiskey they had brought along with them to give some sort of convivial seal to the bargain. No refusal would be spoken, since directness of that kind would be considered thick.

When a place met or exceeded expectations the future bride's people would be restrained in their approval, so as not to weaken their bargaining power. They would bring out the bottle, but since the young man's people usually asked for too big a sum they would get themselves into a haggling mood. The amount of money to be brought in by the bride at the turn of the century would be around seventy–five pounds for a good place, although a big place, maybe ten acres, and a good family name, would command a hundred pounds or more. This sum of money on a market day would buy a fair amount of stock. Certain shrewd families would pay over only half on marriage of the full amount to be given, the rest to be paid on the birth of the first child—for it would be considered a big loss to give out to another place such a large sum if there was no issue. All this, however, is only the bones of the proceedings, for there were many other judgements to be made.

'A great match was made for your mother between herself an' a man beyond in Cahir,' my Aunt Ellen told me, 'an' wasn't it fixed that on this saint's day that was coming up, wouldn't herself and myself go into Kiltimagh after Mass, and himself would be seen talking to our uncle, Pat Mac, and that was how we'd know your man, for neither your mother nor myself had set eyes on him. Now I need hardly tell you, your mother wasn't altogether for it. She didn't know the man—indeed had never heard tell of him—and she was a Yank, but just the same she wouldn't go against the matchmakers entirely—and in any case she wouldn't want to hurt the poor maneen's feelings, but above all she would go just out of divilment, for as you know she was a woman very fond of a laugh. An' of course there was always the chance he would be a fine-lookin' man anyway, for we'd heard powerful reports of him.'

My Aunt Ellen was smoking her clay pipe as she was telling me this: 'Anyway, we got there into the town of Kiltimagh after Mass, and I remember we were laughin' and jokin' a bit as we went down the street. Now sure enough, there was himself talking to Uncle Pat, and I remember the sight of him well, the proposed husband, a stiff-built little maneen, not so little at all but would maybe give one that impression, and he was dressed for the occasion, and I liked the look of him—for he was surely better than the one I got myself that never came back from the hay. True enough, he was putting the style on a bit, swingin' his shoulders back and laughin' away, for after all wasn't he up for inspection an' the poor divil wanted to make a good show of it, I suppose. But do you know when your mother saw him she put her hand to her mouth and whispered to me: "Is it expecting me to marry a man like that!" So I said to her: "It's a great match altogether—hasn't he near a dozen acres of land—and isn't he a fine splinter of a man." "But don't you see," said your mother, *"he has the two tabs at the back of his boots sticking out a mile!"* "Sure haven't you only to tell him to put them back inside," I said to her, "will take only two seconds for him to do it, an' what finer man would any woman want!" So your mother said: "I won't marry a man I have to tell put his tabs back inside his boots!"

'Now there he was walking ahead of us amongst the people that would be out throngin' the streets on a holy day, and he was talking away to our Uncle, wavin' his hands one way an' another, and I suppose he must have felt our eyes on him, for what does he do but put on more gimp than ever to impress us, makin' out he was a great man altogether, that the street would hardly hold the likes of him. Now as bad luck would have it he happened to be passin' a shop where the shopkeeper had set out a tremenjus high pile of buckets in front of the door, and sure enough didn't he give an extra swagger altogether an' strike his shoulder against one of the buckets, an' that sent the whole collection swingin' from one side to the other and the next thing the buckets went clatterin' an' bouncin' an' rollin' all over the place so that there wasn't a one in the street but was turnin' and laughin' to hear the commotion of the buckets scatterin' and rollin' everywhere! "Well whatever doubt I had before," said your mother "that is a sign from heaven surely. I wouldn't marry that poor one if he had a million acres." '

When I heard that story from my Aunt Ellen I found it hard not to sympathize with that man, for when I wore boots I could never keep the tabs in, and if there was anything to be knocked over I would knock it over. In fact I began to imagine this little man as a father I almost had, and this grew into seeing him as the one who missed being my real father simply on account of boot tabs and an encounter with a pile of buckets.

That was the usual and respectable aspect of marriage in those days, but young Irish blood was not always so easily controlled and there was many a runaway match—the February Fair in Kilkelly being known as Runaway Fair. A youth and girl who had met at some dance, but were unable to get both sets of parents to agree to the match, would each go off to the fair and, having arranged to stay with friends or relatives for the night, would get married next morning. (Although matchmaking was no longer common practice in 1945, there was some talk when I was there of a local man, a bachelor in his fifties, who lived alone, and had a decent holding of land, but neglected it and had the animals in and out of the home, of attempts that had been made to make a match for him and get some capable woman to take over. 'Sure it's no good at all,' said my Aunt, 'he wouldn't take any—but as Pat the matchmaker said, "If only I'd match him with any of the young men he'd agree at once—it's the women he can't stand!" ')

There was no real match made between my father and mother, since he had been put to work as an apprentice shop-boy in the firm of a wholesale provision merchant, Richard Henry of Ballyhaunis, at a period when such boys lived in; perhaps for this reason he did not inherit the smallholding, which, it would appear, went to his one sister when she married. The idea of the marriage was merely suggested by Mary O'Malley, a dressmaker in Ballyhaunis and a friend of my mother's sisters. A match in which any woman had a hand was said to be unlucky, and it was she who brought them together. It was arranged that with the savings my mother had brought home from her years in America, a little grocer's shop could be taken over in a village called Devlis and my father would eke out the shop takings with a job as a platelayer on the railway.

# 10

Throughout my school life in Bolton, up to the age of fourteen in 1924, when, for the purpose of starting work, a birth certificate was required, my Christian names had been taken to be William Francis, and the date of my birth 12 June 1910. When the certificate arrived from the office of the registrar in County Mayo, I was dismayed to learn that the official names were William John; not only had I a special affection for St Francis, but it now seemed as though I had been a fraud all my life; a further embarrassment was that of my birth date being 13 June instead of the 12th. I felt that in all honesty I had to stop using the name Francis, but to change my birthday was too cumbersome, and I left it as it was. It made matters no better that my baptismal mug had the initials W.F. engraved on it, but the year of my birth given as 1911. I attempted to question my mother on how such errors could be made about proper names and dates, and the answer I got was, 'Do you think at a time like that people would have nothing else to think of but the date! But whatever that piece of paper says—Francis you were baptized, after the holy saint! And surely the only thing that matters is that you were a sound, healthy child, the Lord be thanked, and created in God's image and likeness!' The answer did not entirely satisfy my schoolboy mind.

Years later I had occasion to send for my baptismal certificate, and sure enough there were the names William John Francis, and the date of birth was given as 12 June 1910. I now felt piqued that I had relinquished the good name Francis over the intervening years, one to which I was entitled, and which would have been a comfort, and I also felt myself to be something of a turncoat. I was much older now, and when I casually mentioned the matter to my mother and asked which was the actual date she said: 'Neither of them.' Then the simple explanation came out: 'At that time the priests made a great fuss that a child must be brought in and baptized as soon as possible after birth —which was usually the next Sunday after.' (I should also point out that families were large at the time, often one child every year, and infant mortality was high, so that the impoverished peasant family could not afford the expense of a funeral if a child died within a day or two of birth. I recall my cousin gently leading me aside when I was about to cross a spot known as The Mound, and explaining that in the old days of the famines and after, any sickly newborn infant would be baptized by a neigh-bouring man—which baptism is permissible in an emergency —and, if the child died, a coffin would secretly be made by the father or a relative, and the funeral would take place at night when all was quiet, with holy water sprinkled and prayers for the dead recited, and though all in the little village would know, nothing would ever be again mentioned. I was told that the spot was treated with great respect, animals kept away from grazing there and no one would deliberately walk on it.)

'The priest would be cross and start scoldin',' went on my mother, 'if the child was more than a week old when taken for baptism. But to take a babe so young was seldom convenient, for the mother would need to be up and around preparin' things for the do, and maybe there wouldn't be money enough for a half-barrel of porter an' a bottle or two of whiskey—an' it would be the poor christenin' surely without enough drink. So, no matter when the child was born, the godparents would make out the date of birth to be Sunday before, just to suit the priest. I've seen children taken in to be baptized, and said to be only a week old, that would be leppin' out of your hands and into the holy water font—if one didn't hold them down! As to the date of your birth, divil a one of me knows, but you were baptized on Sunday the 19th, and the date of birth was given as Sunday the 12th.' She was perfectly right as to the days and dates, but what about the confusion of names?

'Your godfather, Uncle James Loughan, a decent, respectable man, God rest him, went off with Edith Laffen—they stood for you—and the names to be given were William Francis—after your Uncle William and the holy Francis, but it seems that June the 12th was the feast day of some St John or other, and the priest slipped that name in, as they usually did.' (St John of St Facundus: that is the St John born in the fifteenth century at San Facondo in Spain. 'Favoured by the Holy Ghost with a marvel-lous gift for peacemaking, from childhood he exhorted other children to concord.' Although less celebrated than St John the

67

Baptist, 24 June, I felt the choice of peacemaker for me had been a felicitous one.)

But why was the 'Francis' missing on the official birth certificate? And why was the date wrong on the registrar's certificate, it being the 13th instead of the 12th? 'Sure wasn't it Biddy Costello who attended your birth, God rest her, and registered it down in Ballyhaunis a fortnight later, and how could you expect the poor woman to remember three names or any dates when she couldn't write her own name?' And sure enough on the birth certificate her name is stated and beside it X *her mark*. 'And as for the wrong year on the baptismal mug—wasn't it a couple of years later before your Uncle Jim could rustle up enough to buy you one, by which time the poor man would have forgotten more than your year of birth—with all that happened him.' Like most mysteries, that of my varying names and dates of birth was easily explained once the facts were known—the actual date is no longer of interest to me. I have told of it in detail merely to give some impression of the time and place, and the values of the people, particularly those of my own family, and their way of dealing with regulations imposed upon them. Should it create a scepticism about official records this may not be out of place.

The idea of there being a living God, the Supreme Being—'Who alone exists of Himself and is infinite in all perfections'—took hold of me at an early age. It could hardly do any other in an Irish home of that day, if a child was disposed to think at all. The names of Jesus, Mary, and Joseph were uttered dozens of times a day, and, together with St Anthony, would be invoked in emergencies of every kind. Gaelic incantations, more ancient than St Patrick's Christianity, were in constant use, and prayers were said night and morning; one always blessed oneself before a meal, a holy scapular was worn almost as an article of underwear, pictures of the Sacred Heart and St Patrick were the sole decorations, rosary beads were always around somewhere, and holy water always at hand in a whiskey bottle, and the minute my father looked out of the door, whether it was rain or shine, he would say, 'That's a great day, thanks be to God!' At all comings and goings His name was heard, 'God bless all here!' and 'God speed'; 'God guide you,' or 'God and Mary attend you.'

Although I wasn't too happy about God Himself, or comfortable at the idea of His unseen and unheard Presence every-where, I accepted that He would be someone I should have to take into account to my dying day; I almost never approached Him directly, but got in touch with His Holy Mother, or St Joseph, or the Sacred Heart to plead on my behalf, and from these I drew great comfort. I remember the room at the back of the little shop we had, how in the evenings there would be the turf-fire going, and all my father's cronies would gather, smoking their clay pipes and drinking porter drawn fresh from the little barrel he would have in. There was one man, Tom Donelly, whose favourite I was, and I would stand between his knees, and when my father wasn't looking, he would give me gulps of the stout from his mug, and let me take a puff at his clay pipe with its hot, brown stem. My father, angry that I was up so late, would attempt to frighten me to bed by threats and shouts. But I had already sensed that it was all bluster, that he would never lay a hand on me, and I would call out, 'I defy you!' or 'Suff!' Finally, my cousin Mary Ellen would coax me off, sometimes lifting me up in her arms, my senses whirling, and as she tucked me into bed she would give me a fistful of coppers from the shop drawer. Then I'd demand the rosary beads, and clutching the coins in one hand and the Cross in the other, I'd go off to sleep feeling well protected. A true Irish Catholic.

Our household at the time was made up of Father and Mother (we always called them by the proper name, and I never heard my father address my mother except as 'Ma'am' or 'Woman' and she him as 'Sir'), Edward, the eldest, aged eight, May aged six, myself at four, and Mary Ellen, the daughter of my mother's eldest sister, who lived at Knock, a few miles away, and helped with the shop and us. There was also my sister Doll, who was seven, living with Aunt Ellen, and Peggy aged three, living with Aunt Maggie—which eased the burden on my mother and gave the sisters an extra child (which, many years later, they were unhappy to have to part with).

My father was aged forty, a sturdy figure of a man, with a red complexion, thick, black hair that stood up on his big head, and blue eyes that would stare like those of a tom-cat when he was pressing his opinion on anyone (I was not unlike him, with black hair, big head, blue eyes, and a round face, but I never stared). Whilst I was not aware of any hatred toward my father,

I simply couldn't stand the sight of him. He had a loud voice, he was always in the right, you could see from his face that he never listened to a word that was spoken to him—and above all he seemed set on taking my place in the big bed beside Mother. Often in the morning I would wake up to find myself in Mary Ellen's bed, which wasn't too bad, but not like Mother's.

The shop was failing (I was to gather details over the following years, for I had a way of overhearing talk that wasn't meant for me), and it could hardly not fail with my father's liking for drink and my mother's natural goodness of heart; she would refuse no one, no matter what they owed, and how remote the chances of their paying up. 'See that you would always do the decent thing,' she counselled us, 'an' that you could never attempt to get the better of anyone.' I am sure she was right, for how could you sleep in your bed at night with rolls of bacon and cases of eggs below in the shop, and some poor neighbour and her children hungry for a bite to eat. Indeed, she pressed groceries on those who were too proud to ask, and often this caused scenes between my father and herself (not that she would ever quarrel). Then the Great War broke out in 1914, and it was planned that my father would go over to Bolton in Lancashire, near where my Uncle William lived, and would start work in the coal-mines, where they were short of men, then rent a house and get furniture, and we would go over and join him. They all said there were great prospects in England for the children, and lashings of work to be had now there was a war on.

Although I put on a tearful show at his going, and felt a sense of loss for a time, I was secretly overjoyed, for now I could claim my place in bed beside Mother every night. However, in my father's departure I found a mixed blessing, for the day he left for England saw the end of the gathering of men, and the drinking and talking, which I had always enjoyed. My mother was the most hospitable soul one could meet, but she would not have the home turned into a shebeen, and also she had a distaste for drink and drinking: 'There was never luck,' was one of her sayings, 'where there was too much drinking.' And true enough it was to prove over the years. The evenings were quiet now as we began to prepare for leaving home—except the nights when the tinkers would start a fight at the crossroads.

I remember well the soft, grey, December morning we left our little Irish home. They did not get me to go passively. Some instinct warned me against going, against the unknown that lay ahead, and I cried, kicked, thumped, and screamed as Mary Ellen tried to get me out of the house, and finally I clung desperately to the old, wooden door. This was the home of my birth, this my dear native land, and I wasn't going to be wrenched away from it without a struggle. The man with the ass-cart, on which was our big trunk, called out that he would be off to Ballyhaunis station to make sure the train wouldn't leave without us. Finally, Mother told Mary Ellen and them all to leave me alone a minute and not upset me any more, and now she stooped down, put her arm coaxingly round me, and began to tell me what a great place altogether England was—just like America, where she had lived—and she went on about how I would love it, and when we were settled in the grand new house my father had found for us in Bolton, wouldn't each and everyone of us, myself in particular, she declared, *be on the pig's back*. Somehow, deep down inside me, there was this uneasy doubt about that same pig's back. But I stifled my misgivings, let her dry my tears, and, going against this instinctive feeling, vaguely allowed myself to be persuaded. Trying to swallow my sobs I hobbled off along the road toward the station, in the new shoes that were pinching my broad, fat feet. Suddenly, everyone got excited, and began to hurry, as, far away in the quiet distance could be heard the sound of the Dublin train. But I refused to be hurried, wishing in my heart we might miss it forever.

# 11

I remember clearly that train journey across Ireland, with Edward and May sitting there stiff and silent, as was the way with Irish children trained that way from attending Mass, my mother smiling, and myself showing off; then that night, boarding the strange ship bound for Holyhead, a ship crowded with British soldiers. Ireland was still part of the British Empire, and presumably they were now making for the Western Front. But, above all that happened, one small incident stays sharply in mind. A tall, English soldier befriended us, clearing a place for us all on a seat, and even bringing us drinks. I remember him clearly, how he took on a certain responsibility for us, as though we were in his charge, or possibly his own family. I hadn't been to a toilet all day, and I whispered to Mother that I felt a need to go. The soldier took me by the hand and led me into the urinal, which was crowded, noisy, and had an awful smell. I stood by the stall but nothing would come, and I pretended I had done it. But I found I couldn't straighten up when we got back to Mother, and, much concerned, the soldier took me once more. He even stood by and whistled, but that didn't work, then I released my feelings and cried, and that did the trick. I seemed to be there for a long time, but he protected me and told me not to worry. I think he was a little tipsy, for when we got back to Mother, and Edward and May, he pulled out his cigarettes to have a smoke, and insisted on Mother having one. Not only was she one for observing decency, but she would never slight good nature, and so she took one. She looked odd and comical to me, trying to smoke a cigarette to please the soldier. (Later I was to tell of the incident in the home, causing her an embarrassment, of which I felt keenly ashamed.) The next morning we all took leave of the soldier at Holyhead, and the odd thing was I couldn't hold back my tears, I had grown so attached to him. He gave me a cigarette card, one made of silk and cardboard: 'Here's a silkie for you,' he said. It was a most emotional parting, and it seemed all of us were near crying. I put the silkie carefully in my pocket (and I was to keep it for a long time as my memory of the kind English soldier). Then we went over and caught the train to Bolton.

'There's Uncle William an' yeer father!' called Mother as the train drew along the platform. I could see two men standing there, but neither of them was my father. One might have had a vague look of him, except that he had a stooped manner, but in Ireland my father always had his shoulders back and his hatless head, with its thick, dark hair half turned to the sky. This man wore an odd sort of cap, and his face below it was pale and lean, while my father's face was fresh and ruddy. We got out of the train. 'Will you go across an' kiss an' welcome your father!' whispered Mother to us. So, the man was my father after all! It was hard to believe. I went over to him, a shade hesitantly: 'Father—' I said. 'Willyeen!' he said. I kissed him, and although the voice was the same I felt I hardly knew him. He had taken his cap off, either from good manners or for comfort, and the once grand head of black hair was flattened and grey. Also he had a strange smell, one I had never before known—the smell of the coal-mine. My heart almost gave a turn of pity for the poor man. Mother turned from kissing and hugging Uncle William, who was her elder brother, ten years older than she, and shook hands with my father (they would never have kissed in public). Uncle William, looking smiling and confident beside my nervous father, took me in his arms and kissed me. I sensed at once that out of the three of us, Edward, May, and myself, he had chosen me as favourite, and my young, cunning mind resolved to play up to him.

I'll never get used to this place as long as I live—this was what I continued to feel about Bolton of 1914 during those first weeks. (I grew to love it, of course, and my heart was delighted some seventy years later when a woman who had just visited the town thought it one of the nicest she had ever seen.) Like my father, I was of a nervous temperament, and after the silence of Mayo, where one could hear the creak of a cart-wheel a few miles away, the seemingly incessant noises wore me out; my heart gave a jump every time I heard a mill buzzer blow, a lorry backfire, a tramcar come clanging by, or someone suddenly yell out in the street. The first night I woke up in a sweat from a nightmare, dreaming I had gone to hell, and when wide awake the din went on, a terrible clanging and rasping seemed to fill the little bedroom. I opened my eyes and saw through the thin lace curtain of the window a horrifying red sky—as though everything were on fire. The end of the world, I thought, and I'm the only one to see it! God and His Holy Mother protect us! I was to experience the same sight for many nights to follow, and often to hear loud voices — all from the foundry nearby, where the men worked night and day. Then, while the early morning was yet dark, I was to hear a strange, frightening clatter along the pavement below, repeated frequently, often accompanied by hard, high voices—it was the ringing sound of the strips of metal, front irons and heel irons, as they were called, nailed to the wooden-soled clogs worn by men, women, and boys and girls of twelve or thirteen, hurrying off to the mill to get there before work started at six o'clock, and exchanging lively greet-ings on the way; they all seemed to revel in noise and action, and it was easy to see how the Irish had to succumb to such a bold and energetic people.

Worse at times even than the noise were the ever-present smells. In Ireland, with the soft breeze coming in from the West, carrying the sweet-smelling air from the vast area of bogland, it had been a joy both to feel it on the face, and to take deep breaths of it, but in amongst the mills and foundries, and seemingly endless rows of narrow streets, there was never a breeze, only a harsh, cold wind at times, reeking of smoke from mill chimneys, and laden with hard particles of soot. I had a keen sense of smell—I soon knew every house in the street from the family smell as I passed the front door, miners, mill-workers, the man from Walker's tannery, each home had its distinctive smell—and now the ordeal most difficult for me was to sit on the privy closet with the pail under it. A terrible stench filled the air on Thursday nights when the night soilsmen, known as muckmisers, came round with their horse-drawn carts to empty them.

I used to think back of the way it was at home in Mayo, how one slipped off barefooted to some quiet little corner of the field and squatted down peacefully, and how natural it felt to feel the soft earth against the soles of the feet, pick a daisy or two while at stool, think about life, and perhaps repeat a line or two of one of the songs or poems Mother would often sing or utter around the house, 'One impulse from a vernal wood / May teach you more of man, / Of moral evil and of good, / Than all the sages can.' And then to pluck a little soft, green grass—how pleasant in place of the crumply newspaper—and to straighten up and stretch in God's open air instead of fumbling around in a dark privy closet.

Our little house, which my father and Uncle William had rented, then beautified—as was the term for the decorator's papering—was one in a street of two rows of terraced cottages facing each other across a cobbled roadway. Father was extravagantly proud of it, of the new chairs, and the dresser with the big mirror, of the oilcloth on the floor, the coal-fire and, above all, the gas mantle, which lit up the place in the evening. The novelty of it all—especially that of drawing water from the tap in the kitchen in place of going to the well—had excited my interest at the start, but my true feelings kept returning to the Irish home. The room dazzled one, with the greenish, glaring gaslight hissing away in the evening, the red oilcloth on the floor, the yellowy wallpaper, the shiny new furniture that you had to mind you didn't give a kick against; I remembered how soft the light from the old oil-lamp at home was, and how pleasant the limewashed walls and earthen floor, and how I liked a three-legged stool more than a chair, and the turf-fire, so quiet and gentle its warmth compared with the burning of coal. It seemed that everything in Ireland had been of a soft and quiet nature, and everything in England, from the stone floor in the house and the endless pavements outside it, hard and noisy— even to the voices.

I was a spirited boy, happy and optimistic by temperament, fond of talk, fun and jokes, and between all hopping and trotting I held my own for a year of so. The first six months, up to July 1915, I was not forced to attend school, and became something of a messenger boy around the street, going to the shops for neighbours. I still could not easily follow the speech of the Lancastrians, and this difficulty was made worse by strange words. When the first woman asked me to go on an errand I had no idea what the word meant, for in Ireland it would be 'message'. I used to go along the street repeating aloud what I had to get and I recall standing confused in Denton's cornershop, while the customers debated whether what I wanted was a pint of peas or a pound of cheese.

My brother Edward made friends at school, as did my sister

May, but away from the Catholic school or church, the Irish were not popular, and indeed seemed tolerated now only because of the War and the need for extra men down the coal-mines. It seemed understandable to me that, being strangers with strange ways, we wouldn't be too welcome. At first I was often called 'Irish Mick', and although the expression didn't bother me, the slur intended did. I did my best to change the high, fluty sound of my voice to a rough, harder sound, but at the least excitement the Irish sound burst out of me. I got into a few fights with my street-mates—backstreet actually, since it was there we mostly played games and made fires—but I was no match for the quick, hardy, Bolton boys. I would put my fists up when challenged, but whilst I was standing that way the boy, smaller and wirier than myself, would dart down, grab me below the knee, and with a swift jerk send me flat on my back—very often winded, and in poor heart for a fight.

A week before Christmas, 1915, at the end of our first year in England, there was much fuss and excitement in our home when I got up to go to school, which I had been attending since July. Mother was confined to bed upstairs, and for once could not help me to wash and dress, nor was there anyone to cook the hot bacon-dip butties, which, with sweet tea, I liked for breakfast. Things were in an awful state, it seemed to me, with Mrs Walsh from across the street helping about the house, and she it was who told us that Mother had had a baby that very morning. I was fussy about food, and didn't like to be without my favourite breakfast, or without Mother to fasten my boot-laces for me and inspect my ears, and generally see me off with a kiss, and I wasn't for going to school, but my father in one of his cranky moods insisted. I was taken in to see Mother in bed in the back bedroom, and shown the new baby, but I hadn't the least interest in the baby, and asked Mother when she would be getting up. Edward and May waited for me, complaining that we were late, so Mother kissed us goodbye, and off we went out into the bitterly cold morning, my stomach empty, and my heart low. It was ominously quiet as we approached the school, and Edward ran ahead to the Boys' School, May went with the Girls' School, and, after hesitating, I went into the Infants' School. I went along the quiet corridor and into my classroom.

My teacher, Miss Lennard, had said prayers, called the regis-ter, and was into catechism. She was a grey-haired woman with a face like a cross goose, and she turned on me in a flash of temper at my daring to come to school so late and interrupt catechism. I was in some kind of daze at the unexpected events of the morning, shrinking from the gaze of some thirty secure boys and girls, and before I could speak or explain she had taken her cane from its place between the two pegs which held up the blackboard, ordered me to hold my hand out, and down with a swish came the cane on my frozen palm. For a moment I was stunned by the violence of the tingling pain which seemed to explode from my hand, dart up my arm and flash through my body. 'The other hand,' I heard her say. I made to hold out my left hand, but suddenly a great wail of crying burst out of me—a weakness which I should normally have been bitterly ashamed to indulge—and in spite of myself the tears flowed down my face, and big gulps sobbed up in my chest. It wasn't so much the physical pain I felt, which had been shock enough, but the realization that there was a woman in front of me who was actually set on inflicting pain on me—not a slap in a temper but deliberate punishment. At that moment the door opened and the headmistress, Sister Edwardine, came in. I stood there weeping away with my hand outstretched to receive the cane.

'What's the matter?' she asked.

'William Naughton here,' said Miss Lennard, 'has only just arrived for school—'

'So late!' exclaimed Sister Edwardine.

'Mi mother had a new baby this morning, Sister,' I sobbed out, all control gone, all pride shed, 'an' that's why I'm late, Sister.'

Suddenly Sister Edwardine's expression softened, and she and Miss Lennard smiled at each other, and all the harsh feeling in the little classroom seemed not to be there any longer. I couldn't understand why.

'So, your mother had a little baby,' said Sister Edwardine. 'What was it?'

'They said it was a boy,' I said.

'Why didn't you tell me?' said Miss Lennard.

And the next thing there was Miss Devine, another teacher, and she was saying how nice it would be for me to have a baby brother. And even Miss Lennard's goose face eased a little, and I was let go to my seat without getting the second rap of the cane.

But there was little comfort for me in all their niceness, for I felt humiliated to have revealed my inner feelings before the class, and was trembling and wretched at the harsh turn life had taken that morning.

# 12

Uncle William, as I had hoped, made a favourite of me, and I was the one who had to see to it that on his weekly Saturday evening visits he was given a fitting welcome. It was an obligation—and not a simple one. He might arrive at any time between five o'clock and six o'clock, and it was assumed by the Irish way of welcoming that you would know to the moment just when it was likely to be. Arrangements of almost any kind were avoided—it was all left to God and the mood. On dark winter evenings, or when there was heavy rain, I would be posted, washed and shining, on a chair behind the plant-pot stand near the window, watching for the sight of Uncle William turning beside the corner-shop, so that I could give the warning call to my mother, and she could leave whatever she was doing to hurry and welcome him at an open door. My father would be in bed in the front room upstairs, after his night shift at the pit, and his few drinks at Saturday dinner-time when he always put his weekly bets on the horses; Cousin Willie Kirrane would be asleep in the back bedroom, after an early shift, and often Mother and myself would be the only two around—which was the way I liked things.

At other times when the weather is fine, and the evening light, I set off to await Uncle William at the tram-stop outside William Heap's furniture shop opposite Vose's tripe shop at the corner of High Street. I must not forget to turn at the corner and wave back to my mother at the window, I tell myself, for it seems not one of us ever goes out of the house over the years but that she is there at the window, curtain open, face smiling, and hand raised to give us a wave, either of encouragement or blessing, or both. There is something about family customs which, though tedious to a child at times, help create a special feeling of belonging to, and being an essential part of some comforting and secure haven of life. I take a few pins with me in case Uncle William is late, for then I can play at flattening them under the tram wheels. You watch for a quiet moment and then

79

put your pins down on the narrow side of the tramline that takes all the weight; when the tram has gone over them you retrieve your pins, which are now broad and flat, and can be fixed into a sort of ornament to put on your jersey or jacket.

Sometimes when walking along through the Bolton streets and hearing the voices and the clatter of clogs, I get a kind of lonely feeling, and a longing for a taste of Ireland and home. It seemed to me that my true self was not alive in a place where I had to pretend I was one of them, and I would get a yearning for some Irish sound or sight, or above all for a smell of fields and ditches—but no, everything is strange, and in amongst the narrow streets and pavements it is as though I am under some form of detention, hoping for the day they will let me free and I can go back home again and be myself. Not that the feeling comes too often. I stand there with my back to the furniture shop window when I see a tram coming from the Daubhill direction, and square my shoulders, straighten up, and force my hands out of my pockets, although once out I don't know what to do with them; I put on a lighthearted smile, for I know this is the style that Uncle William likes. The falsity of the pose is depressing, and wearies me. The tramcar stops and men from the brick-kiln and the glassworks come clattering along on to the platform, and a woman in clogs and shawl, but no sign of Uncle William. I make to put my pins quickly in place on the tramline.

'Sarves thee bloody reet if tha gets run o'er!'

I jump with shock at the bellow, and dart on to the pavement as a tram goes by on the other line in the opposite direction, the red-faced driver glaring around the side of the driver's platform at me, waving his thick, gloved fist. The Irish do not shout sharply, and it is going to take me a lifetime to get used to the change. I lift myself out of the state of shock and humiliation as the next tramcar from Daubhill arrives, and there is Uncle William beaming mildly at me from the high, open end where the passengers get off as the tram comes to a shuddering halt, and at once I put my big, forced smile on. Uncle William is wearing his brown, Saturday suit; he has a navy-blue, botany-wool serge suit for Sundays. The brown suit is cut on what seem old-fashioned lines, the jacket, which hangs open, has a four-button front, buttons spaced well apart, so that the short lapels are set high. The waistcoat is double-breasted, with coloured buttons, and there is a silver watch-guard with an ornamental drop across the front—he even possesses a second and better chain, a gold one, for wearing on such days as Easter Sunday—and his bell-bottom trousers hang neatly over his stout, brown leather boots, inside which he is wearing heavy, wool socks. He has a stiff, white collar, but not one with a stiff front—which he wears only on Sundays—and a broad tie, a flannel shirt, a green silk neckerchief set round the collar between vest and shirt, revealing an inch of itself along the top part of his waistcoat. This removes any impression one might have of his being any kind of a dandy, without taking away from his air of respectability. (Underneath there is a heavy, wool undervest, fastened up with three buttons at the throat, thick wool underpants, and under the vest a scapular, made of two narrow tapes resting over the shoulders; at the back is a small piece of wool on which is a picture of the Blessed Virgin with the words 'Mother of God, Pray for us', and on the front, one of the Sacred Heart with the words 'Sweet Jesus, Have Mercy on us.')

Uncle William wears a cap with a circle of thin cane inside to keep it in shape. He is not tall, but would catch the eye with his stately walk, putting one in mind of a priest moving out of the sacristy to go up to the altar and say Mass. He comes over to me, as I stand waiting for him at the edge of the pavement, and smilingly kisses me on the mouth: 'Well, and how are you, Willie?' He has the face of an Uncle, quite different to my keen eye from that of a father, and even another kind of smell— although the smell of the coal-mine is also there. He has large, strong teeth, all his own, and often I wonder why he doesn't buy himself a set of false 'uns like everybody else, since false teeth have such an even shape, and are not as fierce as real teeth. He takes my hand and we go off together along Peace Street: 'Well, Willie, and what are the newses?' he asks. 'Mother had a letter from home—from Aunt Ellen—they're all well,' I tell him. 'Father had a night off work on Thursday—he had his back hurt. But he went last night.' I give him all the bits of news I can think of, but am careful to edit them. I am going to tell him only what I know Mother would want me to tell him. He is appreciative of news, and makes comments on everything I tell him. As we go down Back Cannon Street, Uncle giving a smile and touching his cap to any woman neighbour he happens to know by sight, I watch for any of my street-mates, in case they should see me holding hands with him, for it is not something to be done in Bolton, except with a child learning to walk.

We turn the corner at Unsworth Street and cross the roadway, and, as if by magic, the front door opens when we reach the sideset, and as Uncle goes in the open door he says: 'God bless all here,' and there is Mother, all flushed and smiling. She gives him a good hug and kiss, and a loud, laughing greeting. The home is glittering, a new tablecloth on, the fireplace and range are shining, and a big coal-fire burning away, but above all the atmosphere of the home changes, for it is as though Uncle William's presence has brought out something new after a week of our grumpy father. As I hear Mother's new, happy, light voice as she talks to Uncle, with him seated on my father's rocking-chair, beaming round the place, and she serving him constant cups of fresh tea and good portions of the Irish potato cake, fresh from the frying pan, with butter laid thickly on it, and I hear her laughter, of a sort I have never heard her enjoy with my father, I begin to wonder about the man snoring away in bed in the front room upstairs. In the depths of me I think what a pity that such a stranger as he should have wormed his way into our lives. He wasn't even from our part of the country, from Aghamore, Tubber, Lismegan, or even Knock, and those kind of places, but over from some outlandish spot the other side of Ballyhaunis, some place by the name of Kilkeel, and he was something of a townie Irishman at that in his upbringing. We'd be much happier without him, I think; may God forgive me to think a thing like that about my own father, and him going down the black coal-mine every night—but it is true, we'd be happier the way we are now with him out of the way upstairs, we could live with Mother and Uncle, and the home would be in peace, without even the sign of a row, or even a hard word of any kind.

Uncle and Mother have enjoyed a half-hour of chat and tea together, and now Cousin Willie Kirrane looks in from the middle door separating the front kitchen from the back kitchen. 'Well, William!' he greets Uncle warmly, but quietly, and Uncle returns, 'Well, Willie!' (Cousin Willie's entrance would be timed to the moment, so that he did not interrupt. In the Irish home of our kind one developed from early childhood an intuitive awareness of most that was going on in a house, and acquired an understanding of the likes and dislikes of everyone, of the comings and goings, and the moods and habits of each member of the family—which was essential in small, crowded homes, and especially those without a toilet of any kind, as was the state in Ireland; without which sense there would be many moments of awkwardness, especially amongst a people of a refined, not to say prudish disposition. Even as a child you had to sense so much without ever having the need to be told, and know when someone was at the toilet, whether in the cowshed or in the outdoor privy closet down the backyard. As was the case in our own home in Bolton, there were at least six of us in the house, and often eight or ten or more, and yet anyone who had not tact enough to avoid going and pushing the door when someone else was using it would be considered very thick. The tone of the place was kept up as though it had been a mansion with numerous toilets. It was the same with everything. Money was hardly mentioned, for it would be considered ill-bred, nor was the price of things; the only one who would talk about money and prices was my father. Children learnt to be silent over many matters, and not to ask questions, especially awkward ones. It was more important to know how to behave than to know anything else.)

Willie, who lodged with us, was a son of Mother's eldest sister, my Aunt Maggie, a widow, who had had a family of twelve, and lived in a place called Knock, a few miles from Aghamore. He was in his middle twenties, a good-looking man with broad forehead and lean face, high cheek bones, dark blue eyes alive with good humour, a straight nose, a wide mouth with full, clear lips, mostly a little open since he was usually smiling or about to smile, showing a glimpse of his good teeth, and a dimple on his strong clean-shaven chin. Mother would hurry briskly around, making more tea, and bringing out fresh, buttered potato cake. No Irishman would make a move to help in any home, nor was he expected to. 'Will you sit now, Maria,' Uncle would say. 'Sure amn't I sitting all day,' my mother would remark. She had a pleasing Irish accent, every word coming out clearly. This was a nice thing about all her people, their soft and gentle manner of speaking, absent in that mumbling and affected stammering not uncommon in men from the West who are at all awkward.

About six o'clock the door would open, and in would come

the other two Kirrane brothers, having travelled from their lodgings in Westhoughton. Paudric, the eldest son, would be the first to enter, followed by John, the youngest brother, not long over from Ireland. To me the scene always smacked of play-acting, to see each character turning up dressed up, and so unlike his working self. Saturday evenings in most homes had an air of a theatre with the curtain going up for a few hours, and each one playing his weekend role in his finery. I enjoyed the atmosphere of that front kitchen on an early winter evening, with the big coal-fire throwing out the burning heat and flickering light, before the gas had been lit, and the four men sitting around. The younger men would be wearing navy-blue serge suits, spotless shirts, and stiff, white collars, shiny black boots with the popular morocco leather block-toe. It was always a wonder to me how they managed to look so clean and fresh. Willie would have got back home from his day shift at the coal-mine around two o'clock, grimed from head to toe, and after a wash would have had his meal—bacon and cabbage, or a rabbit stew, after which he would go to bed for an hour or so. When he got up he would have some hot water taken upstairs to his bedroom, the kitchen being in use. Now he would have a second wash, and it was a skilled operation, getting clean. Vaseline on the edge of a cloth would be used to remove the film of coal-dust which clung to the edge of the eyelids and to the eyelashes, and various other methods had to be used to get the hands clean. He would scrub his body with a brush, and sponge off with a face-cloth. He was most scrupulous about his toilet and general appearance, and one would hardly know he was a miner except for the pale skin with its blue-marked scars, which were ineradicable.

The three Kirranes looked the picture of composure, perfectly at ease, talking but little, perhaps cracking their knuckles if the interval of silence was long. Men who labour very hard seem to sweat all the restlessness out of their systems, and those men, and men like them, could still wear their warm shirts, heavy serge suits, thick underpants, and wool socks on a hot, July day, and not show the least sign of discomfort. Also, on the Saturday evenings, after a week of six turns at the pit—they were all miners—the mere fact of sitting on a hard, straight-backed chair, was in itself a luxury and comfort. It seemed that people who didn't do real work, and real work was something that brought

84

the sweat out—such people would include postmen, all shop assistants, all servers of any kind, and of course the entire lower-middleclass such as teachers and the like—were all in some way estranged from our people and their feelings, and no matter how cosy and secure the others may have looked in their own world, they were not the sort we would ever think to envy or emulate, for it was as though they lacked a certain essential vein of real life, and would go to their graves ignorant of it. One would scarcely wish for a fate of that kind.

The talk in the home would be of Ireland, and that part of Ireland which was their own, for they would hardly stray more than a couple of miles from their own village, even in the longest talk. Mother would tell all the news that had been in the letters she had received during the week, and after that, John Kirrane, since he was the latest one over, would answer questions; 'Musha will you tell me now—what would Ellen have in the far field?—and has she still the cross cow?' Uncle William dearly liked this sort of talk, and so did my mother, and I would sit there, usually resting against Paudric's knee, for, although I was growing, the Irish would fuss you and have play with you when you would be thought in England too old for those childlike pleasures. What will I talk about when I grow up, I used to think, for it seems that all the great men are dead or growing old, and they all lived over in Ireland! What an awful thing to be brought up in a strange country that would leave you nothing to talk about when you grew up. It was not so much that they loved Ireland—indeed such an exalted thought would not enter the mind—but that they *were* Ireland, it was in the blood, and they would take it wherever they went, for once their two feet left the native soil all that was to befall them was of a secondary nature.

The middle door would suddenly open, and my father would come in: 'William,' he'd greet my Uncle, 'how are you? Paudric—is that you? John—Willie—well, b'jaze, gents, you're in the dark—let me see now would I light the gas?—So's we can see each other anyway—how's the ould geezer, Paudric?—Is she giving you enough to ate?—Well that's better now—but it's not as good a light as it ought to be—the bloody rogues at the gasworks are fillin' it with water. Now that's not much of a fire. God save us Willyeen,' he would shout at me—or rather he didn't shout, but his voice came out so loud that it sounded like a shout, 'go an' bring coal—d'you hear me,' and he would take the mug of tea from Mother, have a drink of it and carry on talking. 'Well if that tea is slow poison—then I should be dead this long time—all the gallons I drank—Willyeen, what kind of coal is this ye brought—sure it's nothing but flamin' dirt. Arra go back an' bring some dacent coal.'

It seemed as though my father was talking all the time, for he would greet someone, ask a question—but never listen to the reply. He could not listen to anyone except possibly those who were in authority over him, such as the under-manager at the pit or any of the priests from SS Peter and Paul's. I always became aware that, the moment my father entered, the atmosphere and nice easy Irish chat would vanish. They liked to talk about people and simple happenings, and my father of politics, the machinery down the coal-mine, horse-racing, and newspaper topics. The next thing, he would slip into the kitchen and appear with a large jug: 'Well men, I think I'll go to Nancy's, the ould rapp—a drink would do us no harm.'

My mother is disappointed at all the warm talk having been silenced, nor does she like to see the big beer jug on the go early in the evening. 'Wouldn't there be time yet?' she says quietly, for she would never go directly against anything my father said, or indeed wholly against anyone's wishes. 'What harm, woman?' says my father. 'Earlier or later, a drop of good beer never killed anybody! Eh, Paudric?' Uncle William has quietly slipped his hand into his pocket and is beckoning toward my father, with a pound-note concealed in the palm, for he is not a man to flourish his money. Although a few shillings will buy all the beer that can be bought in one visit to the outdoor-licence premises, Uncle seems always to have the lavish hand, for if one gave two half–crowns, the price of the beer would become apparent, whereas he always hands out the note—and never will he give so much as a glance at the change.

My father refuses the money with hollow force: 'Arra not at all, William,' he says, 'I have money myself.' Then all the Kirranes dip into their pockets, further notes are thrust toward my father, and he puts on a sort of bewildered manner, as though not knowing which one to take, saying at the same time: 'Arra I'll pay myself for this one.' (This jig-acting annoys Mother. 'If you intended to buy the first round,' she asks him next morning, 'why didn't you go off like a right man and buy it without saying a word—and if you didn't intend, why did you not take the decent man's money without more fuss?' Questions which he refuses to answer beyond: 'Arra go on with you, woman—I know well what I'm doing. I do that an' all!' Which I do not doubt.) Uncle William gives an imperious twist of his hand, for there is never any humbug with him and so my father goes over to him, and with seeming reluctance takes the note: 'Whatever you do, don't forget herself.' Uncle nods towards Mother. 'The Yank.' A little joke from Uncle William, and the atmosphere is right again. 'Och, don't bother at all about me,' she says, flushing and smiling. 'The best in the house for her,' says Uncle William. 'Come on, Willyeen,' says my father to me, 'you can get the small jug an' give me a hand.'

I like going to Nancy's—but not with my father. I hate going anywhere with him, for there's sure to be an argument of some kind. But, of course, I go with a willing air, and walking somewhat beside him up the backstreet I sense he has on his going-to-get-the-beer walk. This is a half-swinging gait, one of anticipation, and with it goes a glowing in his eyes, a warming of his expression, a softening of his voice, and an attempt at the odd comic remark, all held under in the way some men prefer not to show pleasure too readily. I am a little behind him, and again ahead of him, for as he cannot join in a conversation but must go his own way, so is it when he is out walking with anybody, with me, with Mother, or with other men, he is somehow always on his own, apart, ahead, or behind, turning and half-turning, but never quite going the same way as the rest of them, and obviously engrossed in his own affairs of mind and feeling—if with a group, letting out the odd called comment to make his presence felt. My father nourished a form of secretiveness—a peasant secretiveness perhaps—whereas with Uncle William and the Kirranes it was a peasant privacy, a reserved and dignified manner. He liked to wink, nod, and nudge in a conspiratorial way; which they would never have indulged in.

When we get to Nancy's there is a broad doorstep, with a double door, both sides shut uninvitingly; then there is a brass latch fixture set high up on the door, which has to be forced down, after which the door needs to be pressed with knee or shoulder as there is a huge spring arrangement on it inside, connected with a large bell over the door, which goes off with a loud clang as we enter. This warning now brings Nancy out of the warm kitchen. She is in her forties, with a cold, unsmiling face. Although grudgingly glad of any custom, she is not pleased at being drawn from the cosy fire to serve a customer, and lets us see as much. Ma Nightingale, a small shrunken white-haired woman, wearing a shawl over her shoulders, who is the actual licensee of the place, follows Nancy just to supervise, and Jack, the old but still lusty Airdale dog, makes an appearance to see what is going on.

'Yes?' says Nancy, taking a small piece of a hanky out of her black apron-pocket to wipe her dripping, cherry nose. My father draws a deep breath and prepares for the encounter. Every transaction of this kind—whether for beer or tobacco, in a greengrocer's for a cabbage, or a poulterer's for a rabbit, in fact almost everyone he has any dealing with, even if it's only a tram conductor—has the makings of a disagreement of some kind. This inner thorniness has led to numerous breaks with people, particularly pub landlords, so that he finds himself frequently changing his pub—and always a feud going on, some of which the other party may have been partly, but not quite wholly, unaware.

'Well, Nancy!' he says. 'Good evening, ma'am,' and he gives a touch of his cap to old Ma Nightingale, 'it's great weather we're having for this time of the year.' His boisterous geniality does not take in either Ma Nightingale or Nancy, nor do they respond to such cajolery. They don't want to know about the weather or anything else—they want a hold on your money, and get you out of the place so that they can go back to their fireside. Behind my father's back I give a traitorous smile to the pair of them to unload some of my embarrassment. Beer off-licence premises do not appear to attract the most generous of natures for their tenants, and Nancy and Ma Nightingale are no exceptions.

'Do you think,' says my father, putting down the large, white, blue-ribboned jug on the counter, 'do you think could you get a quart into that jug—without me spillin' it all the way home?'

'A quart!' exclaims Nancy. 'I could get three pints into it.'

'You'd never get three *full* pints into it,' says my father, the gall rising in spite of his attempt at control. 'Anyway, try a quart—a quart of best in it for a start,' he makes a second attempt. Father watches keenly over the counter as Nancy takes the jug, so that justice to the full measure may be done and seen to be done, and also to make sure she doesn't swiftly tip a dollop of the drainings into it, which are in a metal container just below the tap—a practice she is not beyond employing. She measures the two pints into the big jug, drawing beer four times using a half–pint measure. Ma Nightingale looks on, and so does Jack the Airedale. The time passes very slowly. 'Make it five gills anyway,' says my father, 'an' that should bring it over the top —*with the pull,*' he adds. There is a custom known as 'the long pull' by which a generous landlord, when serving some old pensioner, will give one long pull, bringing the froth up near to the top of the jug, so that a generous half–pint is assured. But Nancy has acquired a knack of giving a spurious long pull at the end, which simply spurts out a slithering froth, with less than a spoonful of beer carried with it.

My father, now seething (obvious to me from the way his top teeth clench his lower lip) since his ingratiating display has brought him no advantage, now turns to irony: 'Well that's a great long pull you give, Nancy,' he remarks, 'I never saw one like it!' 'The long pull', she explains, 'is illegal.' (In fact, there are to be wartime notices put on show to this effect, and Nancy will be amongst the first to display them.) 'Are you telling me,' he goes on, 'there are five gills of beer in that jug!' 'I'll measure it all again for you,' she says. 'Fill it up,' he says, 'no matter what it costs. Have you any oatmeal stout?' He looks up at the ceiling—anywhere to avoid looking at Nancy, and he laughs, a loud laugh of frustration. At least on this occasion he won't be asking for a glass of beer to drink on the sly as he stands at the counter (one of his tactics to put himself a drink ahead of the others, what my mother speaks of as 'slunging'). I feel that few things would give him greater relief than to put his fingers round Nancy's throat and threaten to strangle her if she doesn't give better measure—and at the same time see old Ma Nightingale collapse with shock. What am I doing in this place at all, I think to myself, it's all like a nightmare, for three people I feel less drawn to than Nancy, Ma Nightingale, and my own father, would be hard to find—although I have a soft spot for the old Airedale, Jack, who is frequently involved in street scenes owing to his weakness for getting himself fastened to young bitches. I cannot but think of the rare visits I have made with Uncle William to Nancy's when she and old Ma Nightingale simply bloom under his gracious approach, and actually invite us into their cosy little front kitchen going as far as to offer a cup of tea, and, into the bargain, Uncle buys me a bag of sweets; or, better still, when I go with Cousin Willie Kirrane, and Nancy becomes a giggling and blushing girl, so much unlike her ordinary self that the knack of the frothy pulls fails her and she actually gives some extra beer for nothing. Also, I get twopence or threepence from Willie out of the change.

We are scarcely out of the place before my father half turns to me, 'God forgive me, Willyeen,' he sighs, 'but that one is a thick, ignorant, mean bitch. Did you see the extra she gave me—the long pull—a bloody ould blob of froth. She has the two meanest hands I ever laid eyes on—an' may they drop off if ever she pulls me another pint!' He stops to draw his breath and to give more weight to his words: 'An' did you see the other ould rapp—watchin' for fear I'd get one drop too much. Arra if they had that pair over in Ireland sure they'd march them out an' shoot them! They've taken the good out of the beer. Even the bloody ould dog was watching. The divil melt the lot of them. I'll never set foot in there for another drink—and that's a big thing to say. I've a good mind to write to Magee's brewery and have the pair of them put out on to the street. It would be the bloody price of them for their dirty, mean way of treating the public.'

I wonder, as we go along the backstreet, with myself carrying the smaller jug of beer, how it is that with all the millions of men in the world I should have this certain one for my father. And yet, even at that age, I had come to accept that there was no use at all in appraising one's father as to good or bad, any more than God above, since the father was the father, and he could be no other than he was, and as his nature would let him be. There was something utterly final about a father, he could never be changed for another, or got free of, but would remain the son's father to the end of his days. And no matter what you may think, you can't escape a feeling that somehow you owe your own father something which you'll never be able to repay—you owe him life itself. And underneath the dislike and frustration and other feelings there's a funny little impulse inside often trying to come out, one that feels like love.

# 13

There is a vivid pocket of memory left me from what a year or two later I would recall with embarrassment as being my 'wild self'—the self before a child in the Catholic faith reaches what he is told is 'the age of reason' and is considered capable of making his First Communion. I had grown to hate and fear that Infants' School of SS Peter and Paul in Pilkington Street—and everything it signified to me. 'The worst sin a child can commit,' Sister Edwardine repeatedly told the class, 'is disobedience. God finds it very hard to forgive an act of disobedience, no matter how small—since it is your own fault for not doing what you have been told to do.' This meant you had always to be in time for school, you never uttered a word once the bell rang for playtime to stop, you always sat up straight in your school desk, you never yawned, and you did exactly what teacher told you. 'Lucifer,' she went on, 'was sent out of heaven and thrust down in hell for disobedience, and Adam and Eve were turned out of the Garden of Eden, which gives you some idea of what a terrible sin disobedience is.'

It seemed that some shred of defiance clung to me, and in the home I would not give way to May or Edward, and forced my will on my mother—she never gave in so much as apparently set herself to see a conflict my way, as it were, after which concession I was willing to see it from her side; this latter would often be a question as to what I should eat—I detested all fatty foods with the exception of dipped butties—or what I should wear, and almost never would I put on a cap, which every other boy wore in those days. My father, with his temper, I had to avoid upsetting in any way during the week, but when it came to the weekend, with the usual gathering of the Kirrane brothers and Uncle William—and later more of our Irish cousins—I would defy him, and, taking refuge between Uncle William's knees, refuse to go to bed when he told me, and grig him with bold looks from my secure spot, all of which Uncle seemed to enjoy. The school authorities, however, with the exception of the huge and smiling Canon Holmes, kindly and understanding to every child, insisted on total and cowardly submission. And even when you were prepared to shut out what spark of pluck you had left in you—leaving yourself open to tears or other indignities of the softy—it still wasn't enough, you were bound to be caught out doing some wrong of which you had no notion. The sense of anxiety this set going in me was the most pressing of all burdens.

I remember standing in the classroom, along with the six rows of other boys and girls at a singing lesson, shortly before four o'clock, which would be time for prayers and going home. Sister Edwardine was supervising our singing lesson, as we all sang, 'Three fishers went sailing away to the west, / Away to the west as the sun went down . . .'—a moaning sort of song it was: 'Someone is singing flat,' she said, 'who is it?' Singing *flat*, I thought, what can she be talking about? She began to scout around for the flat singer, stooping her ear to the open mouths, and I began to feel apprehensive, when suddenly I felt something hit me on the side of my head that set stars spinning before my eyes: 'You dolt,' she hissed, 'it's you!' My heart danced sickly in my breast from the shock, and for the next hour my head felt out of shape. To witness violence done to others pained me, but when I was the victim it seemed to stun me.

What bewildered me further was the unexpected attitude of teachers toward children at all times. I had been fortunate enough to have cherished an illusion that everybody liked me, and had felt that most people would be nice and kind to you simply because you were a child—personally I hadn't a high opinion of children in general—but once you set foot within the school gate with its narrow, ugly passageway, it seemed that because you were a child you had to be disapproved of, watched, and corrected. You became aware of the hostile atmosphere at once, and were guarded in all you said and did; but what I found most disturbing was the unsmiling face of the teachers. They gave you no response except for the fixed, severe look. It seemed that a half–dozen teachers' pets might escape this, children from the best families, but the rest of us, the ones who somehow didn't belong to a recognized group, many whose clothes might be ragged, the front of their faces washed in such a way that made it clear that ears and neck were untouched—which same neck would often be freckled with fleabites—from the moment they entered school they were in for it. 'They go on about the babe in the manger,' I used to think, 'the Infant Jesus, but I'll bet he was covered with fleabites—and short shrift he would've got if he came to this school!' There was no doubt but that I, in spite of the clothes I wore, and mostly shoes in place of the cheaper clogs, belonged in breeding and spirit to this lowly group. The names had an Irish ring—the Murphys, MacCormacks, Feeneys, Laffertys, O'Hagans, and also the Swarbricks and Smiths to make up the English poor. Although I might be said to be among the top few of our lot, I had no desire to get in amongst the other group, the élite ones, those who sat in the front row nearest teacher, and who would identify with her, and gaze on the ones who were being caned with cool disapproval, touched with curiosity as to what it felt like. What most distinguished such boys and girls from the rest of us was the look of settled security on their faces, compared with the vulnerable look on our own, often furtive or guilty, unlikely to endear. That snug, cool, and assured expression tended to set, producing a fixed look, rather dull, but infinitely desirable to those who lacked it. And this mien—if I may so describe it—had not been acquired so much as inherited; true that even from the cradle they had observed this rather superior look on their parents, and had had no reason not to assume it, but it seemed that they had even been born with a physiognomy disposed to it. None of us others could quite have cultivated such an expression; to the native it was instantly recognizable, you could even spot it in a swimming pool—and by the tone of voice it was emphasized. Already the social segregation had begun; among them were the future lower-grade civil servants, department managers, spinning room overlookers, engineers and tradesmen, whilst we were destined to be coal-miners, general labourers, hod-carriers, and unemployed. Not, it must be added, that they could be in any way censured for it; they were jolly good people, civil, considerate, and hardworking—few there are who do not take advantage of a fortunate class inheritance.

I got up to go to school one morning, and found my legs to be stiff and painful. May and Edward went off to school, and I was hanging back, sensing that Mother would not press me to go, when who should arrive at our home unexpectedly but Uncle

William. It was springtime and he had brought a small bag of soil with him from the farm, and a few plants; he was set on making a little flower garden for Mother in our backyard, a vain hope, where never a ray of sunshine could reach. He had been working the night before, and was wearing an old suit and a scarf. I was glad to see him, for I was sure he would understand. But somehow he didn't; the pain in my legs was so real that I found it alarmed me, and left me without my usual skill at putting on an act. Uncle said I must go to school, for it would be an awful thing if the school board—the attendance officer—who was said to be a spiteful man, ever summoned us on account of my missing school. Between himself and Mother they ushered me out of the house and I hobbled to the street-corner and Mother waved me off with Uncle William behind her.

I got round the corner, but the feeling of painful stiffness did not lift, and I began to feel alarmed, so that when I came to a little window beside a lamp-post at the side of Denton's corner-shop, I sat down on the low sill. I did not wish to do so, looking conspicuous at that early hour, but the manner in which I had to walk would be likely to draw even more attention. Then, a neighbour of ours came along, a Mrs Edge, who lived on the opposite side of the street, and she said to me, 'What's the matter, Willie, love?' 'Mi legs is painin' me, ma'am,' I said. I can see the scene as clear as anything I am ever likely to see in my mind, a respectable woman in her shawl, blue skirt, and clogs, myself resting back on the windowsill, never done harm to anyone and they were sending me off to school crippled. Then along came another neighbour, in clogs and shawl, Mrs Whittle, who lived at the end house, short, stout, a bit wheezy, took in washing, had two daughters, Emma and Martha ('Can your Ebba, swibba in a tubba like our Martha?' the older lads used to kid Emma). 'Wut's up?' asked Mrs Whittle. 'It's little Willie,' said Mrs Edge, 'he's warchin' in his legs—must be rheumatism.' I felt my heart fill with thankfulness when I heard that word 'rheumatism'—nor did I object to 'warchin' '.

'It's a shame,' says Mrs Whittle. And I cried a little at the way she said it—well, that and the word 'rheumatism' brought the tears. I was still at the age when a child will tell his troubles to the first sympathetic face—a time when simple human helplessness seems to touch passers-by as though by chance it struck the memory of some forgotten moment in their own lives, and they are quick to understand, especially if they are women (and allowing for a few hard-faced ones I'd say the Bolton women were the kindest in the world).

Mother must have had one of her *feelings*—the sense which gave her a premonition of visitors and the like long before they arrived, so that a knowing of what would be going on round the street-corner was easy. For the next thing she appeared, and I was glad to see her, but not so pleased to see Uncle William coming up behind her. Uncle pushed on ahead of Mother and, ignoring the sympathetic remarks of both Mrs Edge and Mrs Whittle, he said something to me which I don't remember exactly, but it was about my being bold, and he actually began to slap me on the legs. It did not hurt me much, but, by the standards of our family, it was a shocking thing to do, and I was so mortified that I let out a flood of sobs—to think that my Uncle William should actually lay a hand on me in the street, and I crippled with rheumatism. The next thing he had caught me up as though I were a small sack of potatoes, and he flung me over his shoulder, and carried me kicking and crying off to school through the streets, with Mother following and protesting, and in a distressed state. Up there on his shoulder I felt I had never been so put to shame in my life, and not by the stranger but by one of my own.

Uncle William was not to get me to school. There was something in my nature—and still is I suppose—which, when driven to a certain pitch, would sooner see me die than give in. I think it has seen me through some hard moments, and it did not fail me then. He carried me across Birkdale Street, down along Can Row, across Cannon Street, and round the corner of Thomas's Mill and up Thomas Street, past Rag Bob the barber, and as far as the bit of spare ground near the ropewalk warehouse—altogether not so far as it might sound. But the sight of a man carrying a crying boy on his shoulder was not likely to pass unnoticed in Bolton of that day, for it was during that silent period which fell upon the streets just after nine o'clock when the schools had taken in. Up there on his shoulder I was aware of Uncle William smiling to the women he passed and trying to joke the thing off, but the news of what he was about—forcing a helpless little lad with rheumatic pains to go to school—was travelling along the street grapevine, being supplied loudly at source from Mrs Whittle and Mrs Edge, and then being repeated by other women along the streets to those who hurried to their doors further on, and in spite of Uncle William's smile, it was clear from the loud calls that followed us that he was incurring strong social disapproval: 'Put t'lad down!' 'You can see he's i'pain!' and 'I've got a good mind to report you to the cruelty inspector!'

My poor mother was in a dilemma between respected brother and suffering son, for she must have seen Uncle's embarrassment, and sensed my pain. Oddly enough, the kicking and the sense of being carried in the air, together with the excitement, had eased the pain. The helpless, frightened spasm that I first felt when he flung me over his shoulder had gone, and despite the humiliation of being carried so rudely along the streets, the spirit in me came to life, encouraged by the sympathy of the neighbours, I was determined that whatever happened they would not get me into school on that day. (The *they*, I felt, were Uncle William and those others who had power over me, but no understanding of me. So often in my life it has been that sudden spurt of temper, evoked by what I've taken to be injustice and forced indignity, that has delivered me from persons I was seemingly dependent on, and situations or employment without which it would appear I could not survive—and always, after initial hardship, the change has been for the good, the loss a gain.)

Finally, the spectacle proved too much for Uncle William, and he had to accept defeat. He put me down very gently at the spare ground beside the ropewalk—there was the smell of fresh ropes and the pungent grease that went into their making, and there I cried bitterly and defiantly, and refused to be comforted by him or even by Mother. Indeed I could see that the poor man was sorry for what he had done. But, having won the round, I had enough childlike intuition to refuse to allow the adults to make it a draw, and return to the state of affairs before the conflict; I was the injured party and I was going to let them both see, and hear, that injustice had been done. The fact was, I was a nervous child, deeply disturbed by all that had taken place, and above all the feeling that I couldn't trust my own uncle, or rely wholly on my mother, and that I had been involved in some form of public disgrace, here, in England, amongst strangers. I found that I could not stop crying, and began to feel the retching, gulping sobs that seemed to turn my stomach over, before allowing relief to flood quietly in.

Mother was sorely troubled, and Uncle William got a feeling of my upset state, for he seemed to accept defeat graciously, as, slowly and stumblingly, I made my way back home, with the pair of them in attendance, some yards clear of me. It is a curious thing about all conflicts between adults and children, that finally, no matter how well-motivated the adult is, if he or she is at all a feeling person, he or she must accept being in the wrong, if there is a wrong. The child is moved by feelings and impulses the adult does not understand, and we must respect the force of Nature, or the whisper of God in him. And so nothing but true love and kindness have a real meaning in such a situation. Looking back on it now, I feel it to be one of those oddly significant moments of childhood, that conflict and the walk home, the true meaning of which will come only many years later—if at all—but in which, even at the time, the child is vaguely and uneasily aware that things of a deeper importance are somehow taking place. I think that why I recall it all so clearly is because it manifested some qualities of my true nature —which has never changed, for as I say, it is the same today. I will not back down when I am convinced I am in the right— although I am prepared to lose (which usually happens, I find, when one has trouble with institutions and authorities).

# 14

This chapter was written at a time when I recalled with especial vividness a happening from childhood. I almost always put aside any writing I happen to be working on so as to capture such memories when they are fresh. I drafted it in a short-story form and called it 'The Ran Boys' Dance.' When it was finished I decided it was so personal that I did not wish to impose it on others. I came across it by chance when writing this book, and since I had used all the proper names, and as it was as true as I could recall, and has much factual detail, I decided to put it in here exactly as it was written.

Christmas night of 1916, lying in bed, feeling that Christmas was as good as over, I began to think about the feast days that lay ahead, the Circumcision in a week's time, and a week later the Epiphany, when suddenly I realized that the very next day, 26 December, was St Stephen's Day. And there came to my mind a memory of an Irish custom belonging to that day back home in Ireland. I remembered it as a right merry custom, and I couldn't but wonder how I had almost forgotten such a happening, even though our life in Lancashire did seem to blot out most things of the past. An idea came to me, and I turned to tell my sister May, who slept beside me at the foot of the bed, for though I didn't find her the best one in the world to talk to, I felt the need to tell somebody. But just then my Brother Edward, who was eleven and slept at the top of the bed, started talking about something or other, and May joined in, and during this conversation something warned me against telling either of them. I remembered a saying of my mother's about how no good ever came out of a thing that was much talked about, and so, not without effort I managed to keep silent, and went to sleep that night with this Irish memory warm in my mind, together with the secret resolve I had made, having first asked St Anthony to see that I wouldn't forget it by morning.

When I woke up, the thoughts of the night before came back

to me, but now there was a feeling of stale excitement about them, and all the lovely promise seemed to have faded away. That's what always happens the morning after, I told myself, so don't be put off by it. From the foot of the bed I could see out of the window, and there was this misted greyness stuck there, and the clank of the clogged feet of mill-workers along the street sounded muted down by fog—returning to work on Tuesday after their single-day Christmas holiday. I got out of bed, blessed myself, then, seeing that my father was in the big bed asleep, I didn't go down on my knees, but explained to God that I'd sooner say my prayers when I was sitting alone out in the petty. I pulled on my trousers, tucked in my shirt and put my braces over my shoulders, then went barefoot downstairs, opened the back door and hurried down the small, flagged backyard, mostly on my toes, to keep out some of the fierce, damp cold that was on the ground. I carefully opened the door of the privy closet, went in, and there I said my prayers as I had promised, and as best I could sitting down. Although it didn't seem just the right kind of day for what I had in mind, the keeping silent had bolstered up my will, and I was determined that nothing would put me off. I decided that I would wait until I had Mother alone in the house, and then broach the matter and see what she thought. I went up the yard and into the back kitchen, and Mother must have heard me for she came in out of the front kitchen.

'God save us,' she said, 'were you down the yard in your bare feet'een!'

'Mam,' I said, 'will it be all right if I have a big wash at the tap?'

She gave some sort of a sigh. 'I suppose so,' she said, 'but will you stand on the mat itself, for it near takes the sight from my eye to see you standing on that stone floor.' In a way I preferred the cold of the stone-flagged kitchen floor to the prickliness of the mat, but to please her I stood on it. She began to lay down some old newspapers so as to catch the splashing, and then she crept upstairs and silently closed the bedroom door, for although my father hated noise, he was a man who didn't want to miss anything and he liked the bedroom door kept open.

I took off my shirt and hung it over the mangle. This elaborate washing was something I always enjoyed, and especially on mornings when I had the traces of night-sweat on me after all my wild dreams. But it was seldom I got the opportunity, for there would be a run on the slopstone most mornings, and a swift wipeover with the flannel was as much as I got chance of. I found it a tricky business, washing without making a mess, for the slopstone itself was a large, oblong stone having sides about three inches deep, and a small hole to let the water run away. If I let the tap run, the water nearly always splashed out onto the floor, even though I placed the scrubbing-brush at an angle on the inner side of the slopstone to catch the water and break the fall, and often I'd have a dishcloth put under the brush. I could of course wash myself in the enamel bowl on the slopstone as others did, but that wasn't as freshening or as much fun as the feeling of cold water running straight on my head. And since the bowl was fairly deep-sided, and I had a big head anyway, it wasn't easy to get my head between the tap and the bowl without scraping my scalp on the rough edge of the tap. Besides, when using the bowl, the water had a way of running off at my elbows and onto my trousers.

'Now wash away, agraw,' said Mother, 'but try, would you, not blow too much and waken him.' I almost had to laugh at that, for the funny thing was that I knew I never blew, but my father was a very noisy washer and would blow through his mouth and hands like a walrus when he was washing at the tap. And so would Edward. I thought I wouldn't say anything, for I felt she had been kind enough to me. 'Don't attempt to tidy things after you,' she said, 'or wipe up, or anything of that sort.' I didn't know whether she meant it or not, for she had a funny way of codding which you could tell only by peering hard into her eyes, and not always then. I began to wash, and thought how nice the quiet of the home was after the noisy Christmas celebrations, with all the eating, drinking, and talking, and what my father called *jollification*. I let the cold water run over my head, and splashed my chest with it, then I dried the top part of myself. I thought I would wash my feet too, and I got them up one at a time on the edge of the slopstone and scrubbed them, although I found it difficult drying them on the roller-towel which was fastened up behind the kitchen door. The grand feeling of satisfaction I was getting from all this was spoilt by a bellow from upstairs, as my father shouted down something about was it a bloody elephant that was being washed in the kitchen. But Mother was on hand in a second, and put her head round the bottom of the stairs: 'I've just wet the tea, sir,' she called, 'and I'm bringin' you a mug up.' My father gave some sort of a grunt and the next thing Mother was in with a mug of tea and a piece of soda cake on a plate, and she winked at me as she went upstairs, as much as to say she thought my father was barmy. She came down a minute or two later as I was putting on my stockings and clogs in the back kitchen. 'I'll be gettin' you your bite of breakfast,' she whispered. 'All right, Mam,' I said, 'I'll just comb my hair.' 'Sure you're a great man altogether,' she said.

When I went into the front kitchen it pleased me to see that Mother had the frying pan on the hob beside the fire, and when she saw me she quietly put one side over the pale, glowing coals and came across to the table to cut a nice thick shive of bread from the loaf, taking it to the pan in which the hot bacon-fat was sending up a faint, blue smoke, and giving off a nice bacony smell. She poised the bread above it for a moment, and then dropped it in. It made a lovely sound as the hot fat sizzled and ran up the bread. It was my favourite breakfast, dip butties, and Mother knew exactly how long to dip them—I didn't like a strong, fried taste. She got a plate from over the top of the oven, and then carefully took hold of the crusty corner of the bread and drew it lightly across the surface of the frying pan, bringing to the dipped surface the fragments of lean, burnt bacon. Then she put the bread down, dipped side up, on the plate, and came over to the table at which I had drawn up a chair. She peppered it for me, but did not cut it, for I had explained to her how it kept in the flavour better just folded in two by the hands, the Lancashire way.

Edward had finished his breakfast and was sitting sideways on the sofa carefully putting away the metal strips and bits of his Meccano No. 1 into a box. This was a Christmas present Mother had bought, and my father had given half the money towards it. May was in my father's rocking-chair, dressing the doll that she had got for Christmas. James, the baby, was asleep in his cradle in the far corner. I kept quiet as I drank my cup of sweet tea and ate the dip butty. I could see Edward eyeing me, as though wondering what was up with me. We didn't get on very well, for although I didn't dislike him, or my sister May, yet I often wished they would go off and live somewhere else, and take my father, and leave me alone with Mother, so that I could begin what I felt would be my real life, which they seemed to get in the way of. There was James, but I felt I'd be able to keep him in place.

'I think I'll goo off t'Arthur Nixon's,' said Edward, rising from the sofa. 'Aw reet if I tak' mi Meccano, Mam?' He and May had got the Lancashire talk off, and I envied them, for the Irish clung to me, and the lads at the street-corner often made fun of it. 'Oh surely,' said Mother. Arthur Nixon, Edward's mate, had a father away at the war in France, and his mother was a weaver in the mill and would be at work, so that he and Edward would have the run of the house. I envied Arthur very much having a father who was a soldier and rarely at home. Edward came across to the table before going off, and gave me a canny look: 'Tha'rt not giving owt away, arta?' he said. He's not as numb as he looks, I thought, and the best I could get myself to say in reply was, 'Nar, I'm not.'

As Edward went off, the sound of the door must have woken James, and he began to wail. Mother was out in the back kitchen, and as there wasn't a move out of May, I had to dart across to the cradle, stoop down behind the hood, and rock it with my hand, keeping my head well out of sight, because for some strange reason he didn't seem to like the look of me. 'It's bad enough with May around,' I thought, 'but if he starts crying he'll put the kibosh on my plan altogether.' To my surprise he went quiet. When Mother came in from the back kitchen I crept away from the cradle and said, 'He's all right now.' I looked at her, and felt that, even with May there, I'd better make a start somehow. 'Mother,' I said. 'd'you know what day is in it?'

'Boxing Day,' said May.

'Sure, isn't it St Stephen's Day,' said Mother, 'the day after Christmas Day.'

'It's Boxing Day here,' said May.

'Will you shut up,' I said. I turned to Mother. 'It's Ran Boys' Day,' I said.

'The Ran Boys!' exclaimed Mother, 'Troth an' aren't you great to remember that!' She stopped what she was doing, and straightened her back from the slight stoop that seemed to come over her as she went around the house. 'Sure there'll be great goin's on back home this very morning, with all the throngs of young ladeens goin' off around the roads singin', dancin' an' huntin' the wren.' I saw that May had looked up from her doll and was watching Mother. And for a minute I felt homesick for

Ireland myself, as I pictured the Ran Boys, dressed up in old clothes, bonnets, and shawls, their faces made up with soot or chalk, someone playing a tin whistle, and they'd be dancing and singing at every door. They'd get coppers, sweets, and the odd cigarette, and then away they would go, striking the bushes with their papered-over sticks, calling out in their high Irish voices: 'The Wren, the Wren, the king of all the birds, / On St Stephen's Day was caught in the furze.'

'They wur a right daft lot,' said May.

'Mother,' I said, 'I don't think we should let the day pass like that. Now is there anyone d'you think, that I could go and dance for?'

I could feel May looking at me, but Mother seemed understanding. 'Well, divil a one of me knows, my fine boy, who you could go dancin' for!' she said. 'And isn't that a sorry thing to say in a big country like this, when over in Ireland at this minute there would be a hundred homes you could go to and every single one within would welcome you.'

Somehow I wasn't satisfied with her answer. 'Do you think,' I said, coming out with what had been on my mind all the time, 'ought I go down and dance for Mrs Higgins?'

May made some sort of a noise and Mother gave her a look, then turned to me, but I couldn't tell what was on her mind. Before she had time to speak, there was a low, sharp knock on the door, and at the same time it opened, and the face of a neighbour came round the side. She gave a look to Mother, a glance round the room, and then her eye went over to my father's rocking-chair with May in it.

'Where's t'Mester?' she whispered.

Mother pointed to the ceiling, winked and put a finger to her lips. The neighbour, Mary Anne was her name, looked pleased, and said, 'Can I cum in then?' 'Come in away,' said Mother. She came in, smelling of snuff, and wearing an old shawl over her blue-striped working blouse, a shiny dark skirt, loose clogs, and a scruffy velvet band that had some kind of hold on her enlarged neck. 'Gettin' o'er Christmas is he,' she said. "Ello, May luv! 'Owgo, Willie luv!' 'Hello,' said May. I smiled at her.

'A cup of tea?' said Mother. 'I'm just after wettin' it.' 'I wouldn't say no if I wur asked,' said Mary Anne. 'He dun't say much,' she went on, giving a nod at me, 'but he tak's it all in.'

'Won't you sit down itself,' said Mother, as she poured the

tea. 'Nay, I murn't,' said Mary Anne. She took the tea. 'Ta,' she said. 'James Forrest is missing—yu' know, next t'end house at top of t'street.' 'The Lord save us,' said Mother, 'the poor woman.' We knew the Forrest family well, apart from ourselves and the Walshes, the only Catholic family in the street. 'Well, we all know what "missing" means,' said Mary Anne. 'Fotched her word this mornin' they did. Mrs Birtwhistle just told me. Bonny lad he wur too, just turned twenty. Accordin' to t'papers, Kaiser Bill's finished. 'Course they said that last year.' She stood and drank her tea. 'It durn't stand thinkin' about,' she said. 'I say, before I forget, you couldn't spare me a bit o' sugar, could you? I've run out—rations went—an' shops bein' shut,' and from some big pocket down the side of her skirt she brought out a cup.

'But surely,' said Mother, taking the cup and going across to the cupboard. For some reason I could never understand, she seemed fond of Mary Anne, or at least she never said anything against her. Maybe she was glad to find there were poor in England as well as in Ireland. I saw her take up a large, blue sugar bag and fill the cup to overflowing.

'Art' yettin' th'oon?' said Mary Anne.

'What's that, ma'am?' asked Mother, as she brought the cup across.

'She wants to know,' said May in a loud voice, 'are you heating the oven.'

'I've got a pork pie for yon chap an' our Sammy,' said Mary Anne, 'when they get whum at dinnertime. I could give it 'um cold, but if yu' wur yettin' th'oon you could give it a turn for me. I'm a bit short u'coal. I mean if it's not puttin' you out.'

'Arra, how put me out,' said Mother. 'Here's your sugar.'

'Ee, ta very much,' said Mary Anne, draining her tea-cup and putting it down on the table and taking the cup filled with sugar from Mother. 'I'll hatta go careful I don't sheed it. I'd best be off now—I've got to make a bundle up and pay a visit to Uncle's'—she winked at Mother—'he closes at dinnertime today.' She held out the cup of sugar as she stood beside the door. 'I'll see you get it back,' she said, and she carefully tucked it out of sight under her shawl and went off into the street, closing the door behind her.

'Aye,' said May, 'when Nelson gets his eye back.'

I waited, expecting Mother to bring up again what I had said about going to dance for Mrs Higgins, but she didn't, and as she began to clear the things from the table I could see she had some other thought on her mind. May said: 'Mother, what does *missing* mean?' Mother blessed herself: 'Don't ask that,' she said, 'and above all not in that voice. The poor, innocent lad that I saw walk past that window in his soldier's uniform only a week or two ago. God between us and all harm.'

We were all quiet for a time. 'What would you say, Mother,' I said at last, 'if I went off dancin' for Mrs Higgins?'

'What would you want goin' dancin' for Mrs Higgins,' said May, 'any more than Mrs Higgins would want you dancin' for her?'

. 'Will you once and for all shut your gob,' I said. I made to go up to her but I thought I'd control myself, for I never enjoyed fighting with her, she being a girl, and with this nasty way she had of scratching. I couldn't think why Mother should not be eager that I go off to dance for Mrs Higgins, for although we were not such nearby neighbours, they had become the closest of friends. Mrs Higgins was a short, dumpy woman with a motherly look, and kindly ways. Although she would be taken to be Lancashire, having been born in the Spake Aisy district of Bolton, as she once told us, and starting work in the cotton mill at the age of twelve, yet her mother's mother came from Roscommon, so that she not only had Irish in her, but Mayo Irish like our own. But what made her even nicer than the Irish to me was her warm and open manner, her gurgling laugh that sounded like a girl's, and her way of making fun, all of which I seemed to have seen in weavers and other women mill-workers, who always looked cheerful, and were fond of making jokes. I was her favourite in our family, for whenever Mother bought me a new jersey, or new boots or anything of that sort, or even when I had had a haircut, but especially on Trinity Sunday when I walked through town in what was called the 'Catholic Scholars' Procession', I was always expected first to go and show myself off to her, and she would admire both me and my rig-out, and then go and get a penny or twopence for me out of her nice, little, fat purse. I knew I was getting a bit old for that sort of thing, but it wasn't easy to know just when to break it off.

'It's a great notion, surely,' said Mother, looking very doubtful, 'but I'm not altogether certain this is just the right time to go down to her.'

'Isn't any time the right time for Mrs. Higgins,' I said.

That was what I liked about going to the Higgins's—I was always made welcome. And never came away empty-handed either. It seemed such a happy home, always bright and shining, and they had a canary, a dog called Toby, a bowl of goldfish, and other things that one came across only in a nice home, such as the piano, and the huge aspidistra plant standing in a gleaming brass pot by the window, and often too there was the warm smell of homemade bread and pies.

'But Pat might be sleeping,' said Mother. 'He'll be on tonight, and I think maybe he could be cranky enough if he was woken up out of his sleep.'

Pat Higgins was from our part of the world, but had been in England, and had worked in the coal-mines since he was a young man. He was Mrs Higgins's second husband, which I considered a most unusual thing on the part of Mrs Higgins, for I had never heard tell of anyone belonging to us, or even close to us, where a woman had been known to marry a second time. There was just the one child, Alice, who was from Mrs Higgins's first marriage. Now, although Pat Higgins had always struck me as a very decent sort of man, rather on the quiet side, I had once overheard Mrs Higgins telling Mother that he was very moody and hard to live with. I think she said he was sulky, or sullen. That was one evening, around nine o'clock, when my father had gone off to his night-shift at the pit, and Pat must have gone off too, and Mrs Higgins made one of her visits to us. These were made on the sly, and I used to be surprised at how eagerly she and Mother would talk to each other, Mrs Higgins almost following Mother around as she made tea for them. 'He's all right,' she had said, 'except you never know when you have him. They say you've got to live with a man to know him.' And Mother had nodded in very close agreement with that.

'Look, if Pat's asleep,' I said, 'then I'll only show myself to Mrs Higgins. I won't dance.'

'A fat lot of fun she'll get out of that,' said May.

'But couldn't poor Mrs Higgins herself be busy with one thing and another,' said Mother, giving May a look. 'And on top of it she wouldn't be expectin' you, d'you see, so you might have a start knocked out of her. It isn't everybody here that would want to see somebody dancin' at this hour of the morning. It's not like home in Ireland, agraw, for people have to work.'

'Isn't Mrs Higgins as Irish as ourselves,' I said, 'or nearly.' I felt I must press more, one way or another, if I was to dance that morning for Mrs Higgins, since there seemed no help or encouragement coming from around the home. 'Right,' I said, 'I'll get myself ready,' and I went into the back kitchen.

'Don't take owt of mine,' called May after me.

I would have given her a smart answer back, but I felt disheartened in some way, and I thought it might show in my voice, so I made out to ignore her. For a start I pulled off my jersey, turned it inside out, and put it on again. It didn't seem to make much difference. The thing you needed for dressing up was a skirt, like the lads dancing round the Maypole.

'Did you find anything?' said Mother, coming in through the middle door into the back kitchen. I had been close to giving up, but I thought I might go on if I got her help. 'I think I'd need a jacket or coat of some kind,' I said in a loud, easy way, so that May could hear. 'I wouldn't mind if it was too big, or how big it was, I'd turn it inside out, d'you see and roll up the sleeves.'

'I might find an old coat of your father's somewhere,' she said.

'I don't want his,' I said. 'Anyone's but his.'

'That isn't a nice way to talk on St Stephen's Day,' she said. 'But I'll look is there an old jacket of Uncle William's.' She went to the piece of wall under the stairs in the back kitchen and got out an old, brown jacket and went out into the yard and shook it hard. There were lots of cockroaches around the house and they had a way of getting into the clothes. Then she brushed it well.

'I'll turn it inside out myself,' I said. She handed it to me and I turned the sleeves inside out. They had quite a nice lining to them. Then I put it on. The sleeves were very long, and fell down below my knees. Mother turned them up for me.

'How do I look?' I said. She looked at me and said: 'Musha, you don't look too bad at all.'

I went and stood before the looking-glass on the dresser in the front kitchen, and had a look at myself. 'It's on the long side,' I said.

Mother looked in at me. 'Isn't it supposed to be long,' she said.

'Yes,' said May, 'but not that damn long.'

'It's just right, Mam,' I said. I went to the polish drawer in the back kitchen and took out a tin of shoe polish and a brush, and went in front of the looking-glass again, and although I didn't like messing up my clean face, I put a round patch on either cheek.

'Mam,' called May, 'he's blacking his ugly mug with our best boot polish.'

I took the polish and brush into the back kitchen. 'Mother, I think I'll go out the back way,' I said. I didn't want to pass the street-corner for fear the lads were there.

'I should—if I were you,' said May.

'Is it your clogs you'll be going in,' said Mother, looking down at my feet.

'Aye, sure,' I said, 'they're the best for dancing in. They make most noise.'

'Don't we know it,' said May.

'Go careful in the fog,' said Mother, kissing me, and pulling the jacket straight. 'An' take care would Mrs Higgins be too busy for you.'

'She can't be too busy to watch one bloomin' dance,' I said. 'No one is ever that busy.'

'No,' she agreed, 'you'd be in a sorry state if you couldn't spare that much time. Godspeed, my son.'

'I'll close and latch the back gate after me,' I said, 'so don't be coming out to see me off.' I was afraid she would kiss me again, and that someone might see us, for the Bolton mothers didn't go in for that sort of thing in the same way as the Irish. She saw me across the little backyard from where she stood at the kitchen door, and she waved but didn't speak, and I waved back to her and softly closed the gate, so as to attract no attention.

As I walked along the grey-gloomed backstreet, wearing Uncle William's long jacket, I found myself in some state of wonderment. This was a thing that came over me now and again, when I suddenly lost grasp of who I was and where I was going and above all, why. I couldn't pin down what impulse it was that had caused me to go off dressed the way I was, since normally I couldn't bear to be seen with even a hole in the heel of my stocking, let alone in the strange gear I had on me now, and my face done up, for I was acutely sensitive to Lancashire people and the way they had of laughing openly at one, in place of the kinder, Irish way of doing it behind your back. I felt my mission on that foggy morning had something to do with Ireland, but in what way I couldn't be sure. Whilst on the one hand I was glad of the fog, since it meant there was less chance of being spotted, I felt on the other that I didn't care a damn for anyone. However, I turned up the collar and lapels of the jacket and tried to cover my throat and chest, for that north-country air was as different again as Irish air. It could be damp in Ireland, cold and misty, but it would never bite into you like the air in Bolton did. And it seemed I had been out in it less than a minute when I could feel the soft flecks and even tiny hard grains of sooty dirt gathering on my face. I got out of the backstreet and away safely without being seen by anyone. Then I cut down Thomas Rostron Street, past the outdoor-licence and the fish-and-chip shop. I felt easier in mind now that I was getting away from my own street. I could hear people on the far pavements, but no one saw me. Then suddenly a woman's figure came right up in front of me out of the murky grey mist and I saw it was Mary Anne, carrying a bundle.

'Christ Church on Deane Road!' she cried out, stopping dead, 'is it thee, Billy!' I nodded, mumbled, 'Yes, ma'am,' and made to get away. 'Wheer art' off?' she asked, 'got up like that!' She turned to look harder at me as I went round her.

'I'm goin' dancin',' I said.

'Dancin'!' she said, 'tha'rt gooin' bloody dancin'!—at this hour!—on a soddin' day like this!'

I tried to look round as though making out that there was nothing wrong with the weather, but had a feeling I didn't manage it. Anyway, what had the weather to do with the dancing? In Ireland no one ever gave a second thought to the weather. You danced because it was the day to dance.

'It's the Ran Boys' Day,' I said.

'Ran Boys,' said Mary Anne, looking at me more closely, and seeming to be interested. Then she leant towards me with what looked like cunning in her eyes. 'Know what tha'll be, Billy, when tha grows up,' she said, as though admiring me, 'tha'll be a *buggeroo ranter*.' Then she turned and gave a couple of dance steps herself, and went off laughing in the fog. I thought to myself, I'll go up the ropewalk backstreet and dodge everybody. I couldn't understand what she had said but felt a bit shaken by her manner.

The ropewalk was the name given to the long low building where they made rope, string, and banding. It had been built on a slope, so that from the narrow sideset that ran along one side, you could see right within at those spots where, behind the wire window framing, the window was broken. I looked in for a few moments. There was a strong smell of rope and hemp, and a stronger one of the grease they used on the ropes. The place seemed alive with big women and little men, and tiny boys and girls. The women seemed to be calling out orders of some kind, the men were rubbing greasy hands onto the ropes, and the boys and girls were running up and down. The air outside was thick with fog, and inside it seemed to be throbbing with dust. Folk boasted in Bolton that it was here they made the rope used for hanging murderers. It was hard to imagine that in Ireland it was Ran Boys' Day.

After that I hurried on a bit, and got safely to number 8 Delph Street. I stood and was about to knock at the door when I heard a man's raised voice inside. It took me a little time to realize it was the voice of Pat Higgins, for I'd never heard it sound like that before. There was not only anger in it, but it seemed thick with nastiness. He's worse than my own father, I thought. I was well used to hearing rows, although not a great many went on in our own home, for Mother nearly always gave way and would let my father go on, and my father would seem to run out of things to say. Just the same, even disagreements were upsetting. I felt half inclined to slip off without knocking but I knew when I got home that would involve me in some kind of explanation that I didn't feel like making. And there was this thing inside me that was fixed on my dancing for someone. For a time I stood beside the doorstep in the damp, foggy air, not knowing whether to knock or what to do, feeling uncomfortable, and also sad, for I couldn't think how anyone could ever be angry with gentle Mrs Higgins. The next thing, I heard footsteps and voices coming along the street, and found myself knocking softly, and then loudly, on the door with my knuckles. The man's voice inside went quiet almost at once. The people passing—a man, woman, and child it sounded like—went by me along the street. I kept facing the door and didn't turn. I heard a moving around and whispering, then the door opened partly, and out peeped Mrs Higgins. She looked pale and her eyes somehow seemed smaller. The odd thing was she just stared at me, for she didn't seem to know me.

'It's me, Mrs Higgins,' I said.

'Willie!' she cried out in surprise. She didn't open the door wide like she usually did. 'I was just—' she began. I cut in quickly. 'It's the Ran Boys' Day,' I said. 'I came to dance for you.'

She looked at me as though in a daze, as if she didn't understand my words. For a moment she seemed not to have a real woman's face, but the face of some small, unhappy girl. From inside the house I heard the gruff voice of Pat Higgins calling something. She turned quickly in and said to him, 'It's Willie. He said it's the Ran Boys' Day and he's come to dance.' She heard me after all, I thought. But I wished to God I'd never come. Why do I give way to these mad things in me! I must be a bit off my head. I heard Pat say something about asking me in and not leaving me at the door. 'Come in, Willie,' she said, wiping her hand across her face. I picked up the bottom of the long jacket, and went up the two steps and into the house. The first thing I spotted when I went in was that Toby the dog was under the dresser and not at his usual place on the rug before the fire. The canary was quiet too. Mrs Higgins nearly always kissed and hugged me there on the mat, but this morning she didn't. Pat Higgins himself was seated on a wooden chair near the table, in trousers, socks, and a flannel shirt, and had the look of a man who has only just sat down.

'God bless all here,' I called out in a loud voice that didn't sound much like my own. I knew that if you said that sort of thing at all, you had to say it loud and clear, or all the good would be knocked out of it if they had to ask you what it was. I don't think I would have come out with a thing like that amongst our own, for they would have thought I was 'going on,' as they called it, but, since it had just come into my mind, I let it out. I could see that at least Mrs Higgins liked to hear it, for a touch of a smile came to her face. It was very sad, I felt, to see the signs of being upset on a woman I thought was always happy. I was sorry I hadn't gone and kissed her when I came in, but the moment was gone and I couldn't go back to it, and so I thought I must remember to make up for it with one when I was leaving. I then saw that the greeting hadn't gone down too badly with Pat either. I could see he was trying in some way to clear away from the atmosphere any signs of hard words and the like, much in the same way my father would if Uncle William or Father Fletcher suddenly popped up at the door when he was going on at Mother or one of us.

'Good mornin' to you, Willie,' he said.

111

'Top o' the mornin', sir,' I said. It was no time for half-measures, but I warned myself not to overdo things. Pat wasn't a bad sort of a man, I told myself, but he was rather on the thin side, with a long face and his eyes fairly close together, and his black hair rather neat and wavy, and I always felt that men with wavy hair were inclined to be fussy and difficult if one got on the wrong side of them. And he smoked a briar pipe too, and on top of everything he was a stepfather, which he must have felt didn't have a very good ring to it.

'So you've come to dance for us, Willie,' said Mrs Higgins. She had this very tender voice, and I often got the feeling it might break down in the middle of a sentence.

'Mother said I should,' I fibbed to them, 'on account it was the Ran Boys' Day.'

Mrs Higgins looked at Pat. 'That would be lovely to see you dance,' she said, 'only our Alice has gone to the cemetery and there's no one to play the piano.'

'I don't need the piano,' I said. 'I can lilt my own music—I carry it round in my head, d'you see.'

'Musha how else,' said Pat, and he gave a scornful look at the piano. 'Isn't that the right way!' I felt maybe he was getting at Mrs Higgins, and I didn't entirely fall in with the look he gave me. 'I'm afraid we can't take a door off to put down for you,' he went on, his face screwing up in some kind of humour.

'I'll dance there before the fire,' I said, 'if that'd suit you.'

'Take up the rug, woman,' said Pat. Mrs Higgins stooped down and took up the peg rug and put it out of the way. Jack, the dog, eased himself out from under the dresser to see what was going on. Now that the time had come I felt as though I'd exhausted myself just arriving at where I was, and had little strength left in me for the dance. But whatever was in me made me go on, and I cleared my throat and began to hum a jig of my uncle's: 'Come shake you, Nora, my fine daughter.' I then raised myself up to my full height, looked towards a far piece of ceiling, and set my feet going in the dance. I got jigging well enough, but the fog or something must have got into my throat a bit, for I found the tune wasn't coming as well as I should have liked, and also I found the dancing in my clogs harder going than I had expected. After a time I stopped. 'Would you mind,' I said, 'if I took off the clogs?'

'Why not?' said Mrs Higgins, looking to Pat.

'He's his own man,' said Pat, 'let him take off or put on as it suits him.'

I took them off and set myself for the dance once more, head upraised and shoulders back. The dog seemed to have edged out a bit. I started humming and then began to dance. I felt much lighter and freer without the clogs, but Uncle William's jacket was no help. However, since it was very much part of the whole thing I didn't take it off. I had never realized what a serious business dancing can be on a cold, foggy morning, and I found myself losing my concentration and going into *The Wind that Shook the Barley*, and out of that into *Mrs McLeod's Reel*. There didn't seem enough air in the little room, with the coal-fire burning, and I soon felt the sweat coming out of me. I was half watching their faces for the sign when I could stop, but they each looked kind of solemn. It was all I could do as I finally ended to summon up the usual whoop and flourish that one had to finish a jig with, hands swinging above the head.

They clapped their hands warmly enough, I thought, and Pat said, 'Well, Willie, that beats all ever I saw!'

My courage came back then, for I saw he meant it. 'I'm afraid it was only middlin',' I said.

'It was *grand*,' said Mrs Higgins, 'Ee, you're a little champion, you are that an' all!'

I felt greatly relieved now it was all over and full of thanks at how they had cheered me up, 'Well, I'll be off now,' I said. Now the excitement had gone I felt a bit daft, and for nothing in the world would I have sung: 'Up with the kettle and down with the paw. Give us a penny to bury the Wren.'

'Oh, surely, you must be off,' said Pat, 'you'll have other places to call.'

'No,' I said, putting on my clogs, 'divil a one. As Mother said, isn't it an awful thing to think that back home there would be a hundred homes to go to—and here there is only yourselves.'

'It's an awful thing surely,' said Pat, 'if you gave your mind to the thinkin' of it. Mrs Higgins gave Pat a look. 'I thank you, Willie,' he said, 'for that. It brought a bit of ould Ireland back to me.' And he dipped clumsily into his pocket and brought out a coin and thrust it secretly into my fist.

'Ah, no thank you, sir,' I said, 'I only came for the dance.' He gave me a look that told me to keep it. Although I loved to get money, I was always shy in taking it. Then I saw Mrs Higgins quietly go to the drawer and get her purse out. I realized now that I had gone there for money, in one way, and now was ashamed to be given it.

'Goodbye, Mr Higgins,' I said.

'God and Mary attend you,' he said, sitting down. The dog came out now and went up close to Pat. Mrs Higgins came with me to the door. 'May god bless you for that dance, Willie,' she said. Maybe I wasn't too bad after all, I thought. She gave me a sudden, tight hug and a hard, little kiss on the cheek. Then she put sixpence into my hand. 'But that's too much altogether,' I said. She gave a shake of her head, waved and closed the door swiftly, leaving me outside on the foggy street. I forgot to give her the big kiss I intended to, I thought. Then I looked at Pat's coin and I saw that in place of the penny I had imagined there was a silver two–shilling piece there in the palm of my hand! For a moment I felt the special joy that money gave me. Then as I walked home I began to feel ashamed. I couldn't be sure in myself what I had gone for—was it for the occasion or for the money? Besides, it was altogether too much they had given me. I could feel the pleasure draining away. Whatever I would say about the sixpence to Mother, I decided, I would certainly have to keep news of Pat's two–shilling piece to myself. Well, for a day or two at least. Somehow the deception took the courage from me, and I went into the doorway of an empty house and took off the jacket, rolled it up, and put it under my arm and wiped my face clean as well as I could, then set off through streets and backstreets for home.

The fog was slowly lifting, and I hurried down our own backstreet with Uncle's coat clutched under my arm, and my face turned partly on the ground, for I had a feeling there were still strong traces of the boot polish on my face. I went in the back gate, up the yard, and opened the door quietly and went in. The back kitchen was empty, and when I looked into the front place I was relieved to see that Mother was alone, knelt down on her knees at the fireplace, giving a wipe over to the enamelled hearth tin that was kept over the worn-down hearthstone.

'Sure you're back safe, agraw,' she said.

'Yes,' I said. 'Has our May gone out?'

'Yes, she went to visit Lizzie and Hilda, with her doll,' said Mother. I was glad she was doing something, with her face turned away from me, for that first look from her when I went into the house always told her the things I would be holding back. I went into the back kitchen and hung up the jacket. I took a damp flannel from beside the slopstone, and, wiping my cheeks and feeling a little recovered, I went boldly in to her. She was arranging the fender and fire-irons. 'Mrs Higgins must have had a great surprise when she saw you,' she said.

'I think she was right set up with the dance,' I said. 'Alice was at the cemetery, so I had to sing an' everything.'

'Good man yourself,' she said.

'And Pat said it beat all ever he saw,' I said.

'Urra is it Pat!' she said, with a laugh of surprise. 'Was he up?'

'He was surely,' I said.

'And did you dance for them both?'

'Why wouldn't I!' I said, 'Isn't that what I went for! Mrs Higgins gave me sixpence.'

'Well, wasn't that great,' said Mother, 'the fine decent woman that she is.'

I longed to tell her about everything, the row I had heard, and Pat's two–shilling piece as well, but I had a feeling it wasn't the right time. I had learnt there were things best kept to yourself.

'I'm glad it all went well,' she said, and rising from her knees with a bit of a groan, she gave me a kiss on the side of the face, and went towards the kitchen.

'Yu'know, Mam,' I said, putting on what Lancashire I had, 'I durn't think I'll bother with the Ran Boys' Dance next year.'

Mother stopped, turned and looked at me: 'And why not?' she asked me.

'I dun' know,' I said. 'Happen folk haven't all that time for dancin' over here. I mean they couldn't have been nicer to me, Pat and Mrs Higgins, but the funny thing was when I was leavin' like, the way she kissed me—and I saw these tears in her eyes. It was like she was goin' to go in an' have a good cry. I'd a feelin' it was the dancin' did it.'

I turned to Mother for the reason, since she nearly always knew these things, but now I could see her resting herself backwards, a way she had when she was thinking, and it seemed at that moment her mind was far from Bolton. I heard the front open, and, when Mary Anne poked her head in, for once I was not sorry to see her, for as Mother swiftly wiped her face with the back of her grimed hand, I felt myself almost caught up amongst many strange little human feelings and happenings that I was unable to understand, and I greatly doubted I ever would be.

'I hope your oven's nice an' 'ot,' said Mary Anne, 'I've fotched mi pork pie for yettin' in it.'

# 15

My mother liked to go about her various tasks around the house singing in a low, clear voice such songs as *Brave Robert Emmet*, or those she must have learnt in America, or again it might be some poem from childhood she would utter as she swept the floor; but at late evening, around half–past ten when my father had gone to work, she would be preparing things for morning, such as the breakfast porridge, which would slowly cook on the hob, the fire being backed up with slack for the night, and when there were various extra jobs, such as mending clothes—at which she was not the best hand—she would murmur her night prayers as she was working away. I resisted going to bed until the last moment, especially if I could find anything at all to read, but when she began to pray I found a peace and comfort in the rise and fall of her voice, and deeply so when she came to the prayer to the Blessed Virgin, 'Hail, Holy Queen, Mother of Mercy; hail, our life our sweetness and our hope! To thee do we cry, poor banished children of Eve; to thee do we send up our sighs, mourning and weeping in this vale of tears.'

It was the 'mourning and weeping' that struck a particular note of response in my heart, for it seemed that my own life had become a burden, every day bringing its run of harsh experiences, which had to be endured without a tear, and the world itself appeared to be a woeful place altogether. In the home there was a change for the worse for me, since James, the baby of the family, was now a year old, and demanding more attention, which he was getting, so that it seemed I had lost my special place. Mother would give me a wink and a nudge, and slip me the odd penny on the sly to buy sweets, and more than once whispered, 'Amn't I only placatin' him!'—giving me to understand that I would always be her favourite. (I fancy that if my mother had had a dozen children she could have made each one feel that he or she was her favourite.) With Uncle William, however, it was clear that James had ousted me. On Saturday nights, after Uncle William had had a few drinks, he liked to pick up a large fork and the small poker and make out he was a fiddler, and he would lilt a jig or two and get me to dance when the peg rug had been lifted from the hearth, after which dance there would be coppers for me. But now he lilted away with young James on his knee, and one night he took a pound note out of his pocket and gave it to James. The young baby took it and made to throw it on the fire, so that my father and Cousin Willie darted forward to stop him or to catch it from the flames. But Uncle William insisted that they leave the child to do whatever he wished. The note did not get burnt, but it was a close thing, and as I watched, not jealous so much as abashed, I thought to myself: 'He never gave me money to burn!—and he certainly never gave me a pound note!' My father quickly took advantage of the change, and would order me to go to bed in a loud, confident voice, knowing that without the backing of Uncle William I wouldn't be able to defy him, which I wasn't, and now I began to feel the uneasy stirrings of a cowardice which was much against my spirit.

The relief of seeing my father go off to work on Sunday evening around nine o'clock, looking solemn and subdued was clouded by the dread I felt about going to the Infants' School next morning, and facing up to five, long days of misery. The evenings at the boys' street-corner, where they all gathered telling tales and playing games, had become a new trial, because an older boy called Teddy Fairclough had an urge to make things uncomfortable for me, and my heart would flutter, and voice change at the sight of his huge and clumsy figure approaching. I had to develop a cunning discretion to escape his taunting and threats. The street-corner was the one place I could escape to when my father came downstairs around seven o'clock to read the evening newspaper and to have a light meal—then he would sit in his rocking-chair and drink a further mug or two of tea as he read his newspaper. On wet evenings it was an ordeal for me to sit in the same room, to see him set there in a mood of silent crankiness, ready to flare up at any untoward movement in the home, and cursing politicians and others as he read the news. I would walk the streets, stand in shop-door-ways, and get soaked to the skin just to get out of his presence. The gloom of the war on everything did not seem to affect me much, but what did was the aftermath of the Easter Rising of 1916 in Dublin.

There has always been much talk of Irish Home Rule under our roof—far more than Uncle William and our Kirrane cousins cared for, since their interest lay in small local matters—and Asquith, the Liberal Prime Minister, had opened the way toward it, despite the threat of military resistance from the Unionists, and in the South, the Irish were joining up with the British in the war against Germany. Then in 1916 came the Easter Rising, when 2,000 men were ready to take on the might of the British and declare an Irish Republic. In all, 20,000 British troops became involved, of which over a hundred were killed, and over three hundred wounded. The last of the rebels surrendered on the following Saturday.

Uncle William was shocked that the Irish should rise at a time when the English were fighting a terrible war. Even my father was dismayed—much as he admired James Connolly and his Citizen Army of some two hundred men, organized to protect workers on strike against police subjection, who, with his men, had joined in. Then came the executions of the leaders during the first two weeks of May. Fifteen in all were shot, and James Connolly, unable to stand because of a gangrenous wound, was carried in a chair to his execution. It may have been understandable that in a time of war such drastic penalties should so swiftly be insisted upon, but it proved unwise. Suddenly these men became seen as the heroes they were, and the Irish longing to be freed from England was inflamed. It caused much tension in our home over the weekends. But little as I sided with my father in anything I felt much drawn to him in that. And now the word was no longer 'Home Rule' but 'Sinn Fein', 'the IRA', and 'de Valera'—and it was to be that way for the years ahead. Any time when in school we were gathered to sing 'God Save the King,' I would sing 'God Save Ireland' to myself, and the big pictures of King George and Queen Mary in all their regalia were to me but the images of two figures in a waxwork show, and I would try to imagine Robert Emmett or Patrick Pearse, or think of James Connolly being carried out on a chair to be shot—these were my heroes. What made it all the more difficult for me was that it seemed I had to keep everything to myself: my misery and tribulations had to be masked with a smile and my Irish patriotism with a traitorous assent to what was going on around me. In addition to all this there was the occasional small upset which the child must learn to accept. I should like to tell of just one, which happened in 1917, but is still vivid enough in my memory.

In those days almost every street had an empty house or two with a 'House to Let' notice in the front window, and in 1916 my father decided that we should move from number 30 down to number 8 at the bottom of the street. (My father and mother were to be buried from that house in the 1950s, and my brother Edward, after a few years in America, was to return and stay there until the street was demolished in the late 1970s.) At number 5, almost opposite the new home, lived the Walsh family; Tom Walsh, the father, came from a village in Mayo not far from my mother's, and was said to be a distant cousin. From our first day in England I became fond of the Walsh family, and drawn to their home. I was a regular visitor there, dropping in at any hour of the day, enjoying my cup of tea and a barm cake with Mrs Walsh, and chatting away about everything that came to mind. Apart from the father, Tom, the Walshes were Lancashire, their home had a native character in the way of gleaming brass fire-irons and fender, old-fashioned porcelain ornaments of dogs and bronze horses on their dresser (all of which we, who were strangers, were only vaguely aspiring to). Mrs Walsh, a farmer's daughter, with a lively voice and manner, and a high, silvery laugh, provided Lancashire domestic touches in the way of meat pies and pasties, savouries I liked but which never appeared in our own home, our main meal being bacon and cabbage.

The four Walsh children at the time were Tommy, Allan, Lizzie, and young John. Tommy, the eldest, aged fifteen was working as a little-piecer at Briggs's cotton mill, beside Magee's brewery, where he had begun as a half-timer at the age of twelve. Mrs Walsh called me in one Friday when schools were on holiday, and asked me to take Tommy's dinner to Briggs's spinning mill. 'Now when you've given it to him he'll have drawn his wages from the minder,' she said, 'an' he'll slip them to you on the quiet—an' you bring them back to me, Willie.' I found Briggs's spinning mill, a small one, tucked away in a corner beyond Magee's brewery. I asked a man which was the way in, and he pointed to a big door at the top of three stone steps: 'Tommy works on that pair of wheels just inside,' he said. With some effort I managed to shove open the heavy oily door which swung to behind me. I looked at the spinning mules, and the figures in bare feet moving around, and I tried to breathe but was unable—the air was so hot and humid that I found myself stuck to the spot, with everything whirring about me, and I collapsed in a faint on the floor. The next thing I knew was that Tommy and a spinner were looking down on me, and I was seated on the stone floor at the top of the three steps where I had gone in. 'Tha passed out, Billy, as soon as tha came in,' said Tommy. 'One thing for certain—tha'll never make a spinner.' I made sure I got his wages and hurried back with them to Mrs Walsh, resolving that no matter what happened I would never go little-piecing.

There was a custom in the working-class Bolton homes at that time of making a promotion in the family status of anyone who had begun work. A schoolboy in the home at the age of eleven might be the general mugabout, as the phrase had it, and at everyone's beck and call, but when he reached the age of twelve and went working as a half-timer in the mill (one week the boy or girl worked mornings in the mill and went to school in the afternoon, and the following week had morning school and afternoons working, and in this way it was thought the child's education would be balanced), bringing home a sum of nine shillings or so every Friday, he moved up somewhat, and would not be expected to run as many errands. It was not uncommon in the stricter—and, it might be said, the better-run homes, for family discipline was regarded as being commendable, the more the better—that children were not allowed to *sit* at table until they began work. In the poorer home children could be seen standing at meals because there were not enough chairs or boxes to go round, despite the practice of two sharing one chair; in the home where parental authority was firm a child would be seen standing wearily at the table with empty chairs nearby. 'Oh, Mam, mi legs are tired,' the child might say, 'I want to sit down.' A stock reply to that was, 'Then stick your thumb up your bum an' sit down on your elbow.'

In such homes, however, it was allowed that the half-timer who had worked in the spinning room in the morning should have the privilege of sitting down to his midday dinner. Then at the age of thirteen, when boy or girl began to work full-time in the mill there was another rise in family standing, allowing him or her to sit, and also enjoy such liberties as staying up late, occasional choice in food, particularly on Fridays after handing over the wages, and for the boy even use of an odd, mild, swear word. Together with the new independence went a calculated liberty of giving cheek, which was all a matter of growing up, and had to do with earning money. 'Why should our Albert 'ave 'ad a dip butty,' I've heard a schoolmate say to his mother 'an' not me!' 'Because,' retorted the mother, 'our Albert is fetchin' money into the 'ome. You're fetchin' nowt. So off with you to school.'

This distinction of 'fetching money into the home' also conferred certain privileges on the earner over the younger end of the family and one of these was the employment of a young brother or sister to perform menial tasks, particularly fagging tasks such as going errands. The full-time wage-earner might earn eighteen shillings a week—that would be a boy working in the mill, an apprentice to a trade would earn half as much —which he handed over to his mother on Friday, and she allowed him one penny in the shilling spending-money, which was the traditional allowance. But there may have been extras, when a little-piecer did his own work and a share of the work of someone who was off, which by custom he could more or less keep to himself. So that on Fridays, after his week's work, the teenage full-timer, nearing the end of his working week, and especially if he had been on extras, seemed to fancy the idea of resting back and enjoying some luxury. He would send the fag for toffees, comic papers, a bottle of lemonade, whilst he sat in lordly comfort, perhaps in Dad's rocking-chair if the father was out. The wage-earner would pay the fag threepence a week at the most, but he never paid up in full until all the required jobs had been done. Numerous arguments would break out between master and fag, for the master tended to be tyrannical, sending the fag on more, and longer, errands of a kind that did not seem proper to the arrangement between them, and also he was inclined to voice suspicions that the packets of sweets had been tampered with. Rare was the week that the relationship didn't end up in a row. A schoolboy accepted the role of fag only because that was probably the only way he could come by enough to go to the pictures. Nothing approaching this attitude ever happened in the Irish home—the daughters were the natural fags of the sons—and I found myself fascinated by the clear-cut, yet complex, relationships in the Bolton homes I visited.

On Friday evenings when I went across to the Walshes Tommy rather liked to treat me as his fag. Like most working-class boys who read at all in those days, he read comics, but his main, and most enjoyable, reading was of the English public school scene, and possibly it was from this that he and others got their notion of employing a fag, and the actual use of the word. Allan, Tommy's younger brother, was too near Tommy's age to make a fag, nor was he of that temperament, and John, the youngest, was too young, and Lizzie being a girl did not suit the job. The arrangement between Tommy and myself, however, was a friendly one, and he would be relaxed after a tasty tea, which was always considered proper for Fridays. Mrs Walsh, not being a Catholic herself, had no inhibitions about breaking the Friday abstinence, and Tommy often had a little roast pork with stuffing from the corner shop, or a bit of boiled ham (two ounces was by far the most common portion bought). He would be wearing his long, greasy, mill pants, and enjoying the comfort of having his clogs off in the house, and going around in a pair of smelly, black-ribbed stockings and a greasy shirt, for after a week in the spinning room, the oil and grease would cling to him. He would not have washed—this was part of the sense of luxury and ease—and would wait until his mother and the others had gone out of the way, then he would start going over his spending money, and any extras he had managed to come by. There he would be, swapping the money from his hand to his pocket, checking up on various possibilities, and I would be standing in quiet obedience before him.

'Well, Willie,' he would begin, 'I've been thinkin' it over, an' I'll tell thee what I want. Now think on what I tell thee—I want thee to go to Samson's paper shop for a start, an' I think I'll have a *Magnet* an' a *Gem*—no wait, I'll have a *Magnet* an' a *Funny Wonder*. I feel like a laugh, an' I know one chap I can swop my *Magnet* with for his *Gem*. Hasta getten that—or shall I write it down for thee—*Magnet* an' a *Funny Wonder*? Tha'art sure tha can remember—I don't want no mistakes an' no excuses after. Otherwise I'll send thee back with 'um, so tak' heed of what I tell thee. Now if Master Samson at the paper shop aren't got a *Funny Wonder* left tha can fotch me a *Magnet* an' a *Gem*. Hast got that?' 'Yes, Tommy,' I would say, 'but suppose they haven't got

123

a *Magnet*?' 'But they're bound to have a *Magnet*—it only comes out on Friday,' Tommy would say. 'They can't ha' sold out.' 'But suppose they have?' I would persist—for they once had. 'Now tha'art only bein' awkward, Willie,' Tommy would say. 'I must ha' my *Magnet*.' 'But Tommy,' I'd begin. 'Tha can go down to Daddy Hatton's an' see if he' got a *Magnet* if Samson's 'aven't got one,' Tommy would cut in. 'I don't care if tha 'as to scour the town an' beyond. I mun' 'ave my *Magnet*—I mun find out what Billy Bunter's been up to this week. So whatever tha does don't come back 'ere without my *Magnet*. That's final.'

This sort of talk might go on for a time, with Tommy jingling his money about, and then he would tell me what toffees he wanted from which shop, and would put a shilling into my hand with earnest commands that I should look after it, see that I didn't lose it, and not to talk to anybody on my way just in case. Sometimes he would even see me off at the front door, but mostly he would just wave to me from the rocking-chair, his stockinged feet resting up in the small recess above the oven. A nice lad, Tommy. One could sense the Friday night excitement about the streets, which were mostly cold and foggy on winter evenings. The sight that most fascinated me was that of the Bolton women, the married ones, whose husbands were at war, going off to the pictures in their dark skirts and shawls, and almost every one wearing a man's cap with hatpins in it.

Now on the certain Friday evening I have in mind—and it was in fact the last time I found myself going in to the Walshes to go fagging for Tommy—I got back safe with everything, gave Tommy his change, which I carefully counted for him, and was given a penny, and a sweet out of each packet; then Tommy began his serious Friday night pleasures of reading and the eating of toffees with his feet up on the oven. I was allowed to look at a magazine or comic paper only after he had put it down, for he enjoyed the first opening of it—I was always warned never to look at them on my way back, for Tommy said he had a way of telling if I had done so. If he was in a generous mood he might allow me to go down on my knees and read the back of the comic as he held it up to read the front.

It must have been around nine o'clock, my time for going home, and Tommy having more or less finished his reading, and most of his toffee, had begun to comb his hair, preparatory to having a wash at the kitchen sink. He had thick, wavy hair, golden in colour, and he had put the open copy of *Comic Cuts* on the table, his chin down on it, and in his hand he had a fine-tooth comb, which he would press into his scalp just above the neck, and then bring it upwards until it went to the crown of his head and along the top until finally, with a twist, he would bring it off, and then examine his catch of lice. I was not unfamiliar with the sight, for it was a common one in those days. Mothers, or an elder sister, or often a grandmother would be seen at a window—where the light was best— with a young schoolgirl in front, head bent forward, the older person combing the head with intent patience, searching for insects, as the term was, and on finding one could be seen to kill it by a swift pressing movement of the thumbnail against the side of the comb so that by a quick pressure the louse would be squashed. I could hear the little sharp crack as Tommy put each one to be consumed on the coal fire. "Ere, Willie,' he said, turning unexpectedly to me, 'let's 'ave a look in thy yed see can I find some for thee.'

I explained to Tommy it would be no use his bothering, since my mother had often looked into my head and it had always been spotless. There were some people those things went to and others they never went near, I told him my mother had told me, and I happened to be one of those they never went near. It always gave me some little comfort to know that at least I was free of that sort of thing. Tommy seemed not only a little put out but rather dubious: 'Aw reet then,' he said, 'if tha' 'as none—none'll come out—so there'll be no 'arm done. Sit thee down theer an' get thy head down theer ont' table.' After all, I was his fag for that evening, or at least so he had made it seem, and although this sort of thing was not really included, I nervously put my head down on the table. Tommy stood behind and over me with the comb. Then I felt him put the teeth of the comb on my bare neck, and with a delicate but firm contact he began to force it along up the back of my head, increasing the pressure on the scalp until it felt painful, and then with expert skill he flicked it firmly off at the end—presumably so as not to dislodge or lose any lice that may have been on the comb. He scrutinised the comb under the gaslight. 'What did I tell you!' I said. 'Aw reet,' he said, 'let's 'ave another go.'

Tommy got the comb at a sharper angle as he began once more, and the pressure was stronger, and this time it really hurt as he forced it along my scalp and through my thick hair, never easing for a moment. I let out a little yelp but Tommy was holding my head firmly with his left hand and I couldn't move. I looked up and and saw him looking closely at the comb. 'Hy, what about that, eh?' he said. I looked at the comb, but could see nothing on it but a speck or two of scurf. 'What about what,' I said, 'I can see nothing.' 'Open thy e'en an' tha will,' said Tommy, 'what about that?' And with his thumb he indicated what appeared to be a large ugly speck of scurf. 'Sure that's nothing,' I said, 'isn't it only skin.' 'Howd thy watter,' he said, 'an' watch'—and with that he touched the object on the comb and sure enough it moved. For a moment I was made uneasy, but I recovered. 'That must've been in the comb,' I said, 'before you put it into my head.' ''Appen it were,' remarked Tommy, killing the ugly louse with his nail, 'an' 'appen it weren't. Let's 'ave another dekko.' 'There was nothing ever found in my head,' I said firmly, 'my mother always told me—and she'd know.' ''Appen 'er didn't look 'ard enough,' remarked Tommy, taking a piece of cotton waste out of his trouser pocket and pulling the comb through it, so that there was no hair or anything in it. Tommy had a gentle face and a nice smile: 'That looks clean enough,' he said. 'No mickies in that, is there? Right, now let's 'ave another go—see what we can find.' 'Try would you not hurt me so much,' I said.

It struck me that Tommy was quite an expert with that fine comb—the way he held my head with his left hand and slowly, firmly and smoothly ran it along my scalp. There was this thing about most mill-workers, the surprising skill and deftness in their fingers. This time he made two runs in quick succession, and seemed to cover new territory. Somehow, although he didn't touch them, it caused my ears to feel burning hot. He ended with the usual flick of the comb down close to the paper. Then he looked down and a smile beamed on his nice face: 'By gum,' he aid, 'we've getten two this time! Look at 'um!' With some uneasiness I looked down and under the drone of the bright gaslight I could make out two distinct things. 'But those are not what you call things in the head, Tommy,' I said to him, 'those are not bowdies.' 'I durn't know wut tha calls 'um,' said Tommy, and he turned them over with the edge of the comb and I saw they had tiny legs sticking out, 'but they're damn good imitations. Hy, come an' harken 'um crack'—and he picked the comic paper up carefully, went over to the edge of the big coal-fire, and allowed one after the other to drop in. 'Harken that—an' that—' said Tom. Each one made a clear, distinct, cracking sound as it fell into the glowing coals. I had some kind of horror about lice or any moving thing of that sort, and I felt soiled, shaken and upset. But I wasn't one to give in easily: 'My mother said,' I said, 'that never in all my life has anything been found in my head—so either those ones wasn't real—or else they just got in by mistake.' Tom gave me a long almost resigned look, under which I did not let myself waver: 'Thy mother will be saying next,' he remarked, 'that thy shit doesn't smell.'

When Tommy said that it seemed that my heart sank low, for he had struck close—since it was almost exactly what Mother did say. She would never use indelicate words, of course, but it was like an assurance she had occasionally consoled me with as a small boy when I had had what she called a little accident. 'Don't worry,' she would say to me, 'there's no harm done, for there's never any kind of smell from you. You're so pure and clean in everythin' you do that it's not like it would be with another one—you're different. I'll have you right in a minute. No one will ever know.'

I didn't allow anyone to put the comb to my head again, and I never went to fag for Tommy after that. It seemed that something very comforting had been taken from me in that small incident. Nor could I bring myself to go straight home that evening, but walked the streets painfully aware of the sharp difference between the security of family life and other life. It was some days before I could bring myself to tell mother, for I had to let the sense of shame wear off. And after that I seemed to become obsessed with cleanliness, and would comb my own hair for periods with a very fine comb.

As for dear Tommy Walsh—things were never quite the same between us after that, although I remained very fond of him. Actually, it was only a year or so later that he died. He took consumption, as they used to say, and he spent a few months lying in his bed downstairs in the front kitchen. I used to call in very often then to see him and talk to him, for he was always very nice and interesting. Somehow, his sickness before his death sticks in my mind—for I have seen others sickly and dying in such homes, and although death is rarely without sadness no matter where it takes place, in the working homes of those days it seemed poignantly so. So often it would take place in the front kitchen where all the family life went on, the meals were cooked and eaten, and the family sat around talking, and always there would be the sick person in bed, very often weak and gasping for breath, and the mother tending him, with the sick person saying he wanted something but didn't know what it was. What such a sick one needed most often was probably a little fresh air, because in such homes amongst the dense streets with their thick, sooty atmosphere there seemed to be an utter lack of it. And at the same time the mother would be sponging, comforting the son or daughter, striving to comfort and cheer, in between doing her many tasks around the house.

# 16

I moved up to the big school, as it was called, at the age of seven. On that first morning, as I entered the small, L-shaped playground, crammed with wild and noisy boys, I shrank from the mad tumult around me. The whistle blew, lines were formed, and later I found myself one of a class of forty–two boys in Standard One. Our teacher was Miss Conway, a young teacher, gentle and kind; she wore a white blouse, a tweed skirt, and in place of the stale smell of the women teachers in the Infant's School, she gave off a feminine fragrance. I fell in love with her—not, I may add, as though with a real, live person, but with one from a world so high and remote from my own that I could ever only hope to idolize her from a distance. Miss Conway prepared us for First Communion, explaining how each one of us possessed an immortal soul—I could not escape a feeling that she was talking to me personally and that the others simply made up the number—which, over the years, had become stained by our sins, all of which would be forgiven at Confession, when the priest murmured the words of absolution. In the Infants' School, Miss Lennard and Sister Edwardine had taught of the goodness and mercy of Our Lord, but instinctively I identified what they spoke of with themselves, so that I had received an impression of a Saviour not unlike them, difficult to please and ready with punishment, which feeling I could now shed under Miss Conway's tender teaching. But the truly great sacrament was the Lord's Supper, when, at our first First Communion, the host would be placed upon the tongue and swallowed. Although in appearance the host was a small, round wafer of unleavened bread, she told us that during the Consecration a miracle took place, that of transubstantiation (I got deep satisfaction from repeating such words to myself and feeling a measure of possession, one which could not be taken from me) by which the bread and wine become the body and blood, soul and divinity, of our Saviour, Jesus Christ repeating the sacrifice of Calvary on the altar, now unbloody yet glorious.

I could not wait for the wonderful prospect ahead—to feel the Saviour of the world on my tongue and to swallow and take Him fully and wholly to myself! (*Take and eat ye all of this, for this is my body,* our Lord had said, *Take and drink ye all of this, for this is the chalice of my blood, of the new and eternal testament: the mystery of faith: which shall be shed for you and for many unto the remission of sins.* True enough, we were to forgo the wine and take only the host, but that was of no matter since what counted was the faith we received with it.) Above all, she impressed on us the importance of the Holy Ghost, guardian of the soul, and at that actual moment of Communion—wonderful it was in spite of all the footsteps and movement around the altar rail—I realized what it meant to know the Paraclete, to have Him evermore to guide, console, and comfort me. It seemed that from then on, the irritations and afflictions that beset one in this life—a grumpy father, shoes that pinched the feet, shame over one's clothes, trouble at the street-corner, not having the twopence needed for going to the pictures, and a multitude of circumstances one would wish to be different—could be borne by an understanding of their being but passing states, which tomorrow, or the day after, or sometime else, would all be gone and forgotten, the true life being rooted within, in the soul and the Holy Spirit.

(I remember standing at the street-corner on the evening of my First Communion, with traces of the state of grace from the Sacrament of the morning still present in me, and looking round at my mates, watching two little-piecers seated face to face on the pavement, oily trousers rolled up, the white knees and thighs of each being grasped by the other, as they squeezed out each other's grubs—blackheads—which were speckled all over their legs, from kneeling on the oily floor of the spinning mill and 'wiping under', as it was called, I made a little unnoticed cross over my heart, and thought how sad it was that they had no religion like mine, one that would offer them Holy Communion, that their souls might be elevated to heaven, if only for minutes. And nearby were the older and more pallid spinners, arguing away in a lively manner, and the strong white-faced miners down on their hunkers, washed but wearing pit clogs, and suddenly I felt what seemed to be an immense compassion for them all, my most dear corner-mates, and I trusted God would see to it that there was a street-corner in heaven, perhaps one with a nice fat lamp-post, and that one day we should all be there together—if my prayer was to be fruitful at all—free of worries, blackheads, and all the rest of it, and with a few bob in our pockets.)

Miss Conway picked me out to be a monitor. I was sent to other teachers with notes, and took the attendance slips and the class register to Mr J. V. Smith the headmaster, and soon got to know all the teachers. Although as vain as a peacock I was uncomfortable at being singled out as monitor, did not enjoy being accorded privilege, disliked the role itself, and felt myself to be a turncoat of sorts. Fortunately, with Miss Conway there was not the usual division, since she did not sort out the black sheep from the white. The fact was, there were Catholic schools in various districts of Bolton in which those of Irish extraction held sway, such as at St Patrick's, St Mary's, and Holy Infants', the parish priest usually being Irish, but SS Peter and Paul's had a distinctly English tone, always an English parish priest, and since the Irish tended to belong to the poorer section, the division between those who had influence and commanded respect and those who had neither was much sharper.

After the second year in the big school I went back after the summer holiday hoping that by some good fortune Miss Conway would move up to Standard Three, or if not she, then a Miss Calderbank, who was one of the younger and less severe teachers—the older they became, the more prone they were to use the cane. I felt almost paralysed with apprehension to find that I had been moved up Standard Three under Miss Newsham, known amongst the boys as 'Fat Alice' or 'Fat Ada', a teacher of uncertain temper, who would prowl along between the desks, looking over boys' shoulders at their writing or sums, and if what she saw did not please her she could land a cuff with her right hand as to leave the victim almost senseless. Boys from her class could be spotted wobbling about the playground, the left ear pale and right ear purple. She gave me one look as I took my place. 'Naughton, you appear to have been going about the school like a free agent when in Miss Conway's class,' she said, 'but' I'll put a stop to that.'

I looked around the school and the playground during the morning break hoping to catch a sight of Miss Conway, and get a word or smile of encouragement. Then the news came out that she had gone off and got married. I didn't believe it—I couldn't believe it—that she would go off like that without a word or a sign. But one lad knew for certain. His mother had seen it in the newspaper, and Miss Conway was now Mrs King. I felt desolate that she could have deserted me in such a seemingly heartless way, without even a word of her intentions, and could not conceive that with my thinking of her so much she could live without thinking of me at all. 'She must know how I feel about her,' I thought, 'she must be missing me.' I was not to set eyes on Miss Conway again for forty years. I wrote a television play, *June Evening* for the BBC, which was about our street in Bolton (*Coronation Street* which began nine months later, was taken from it, even to the very name, Albert Tatlock, of my main character), and this brought me many letters, among which was one which began, 'Dear Mr Naughton, I wonder can you be my Billy Naughton—who was in my class in 1917?' I loved that 'my Billy Naughton', and arranged a meeting, and there she was at her local station waiting for me as I got off the train. It was a joy to me at the age of forty–seven to embrace her and give her the kiss I had waited for all those years. And it gratified me to see that her skin was as fresh—or almost—as it had been, and her eyes as blue, and the voice as gentle and sweet. I should have known her had I met her anywhere.

The urge in me to indulge the vein of inner life which had been kindled by Miss Conway and the sacraments, resisted all the religious teaching from Miss Newsham, since the preceptor or priest who fails to attract affection and respect will not inspire a love of God in the young—and at best will only arouse some paltry fear, soon to be set aside. If we are so at variance in all else, I felt, how can we possibly be one in God? But this rejection of taught religion made me cling only more preciously to that which had already become part of me, and in time I cultivated a practice by which I could handle the incompatible elements; during catechism, as religious instruction lesson was called, I would take in what Miss Newsham was telling us purely with my memory, so as to be ready to trot out replies to any questions that might follow, but detaching what I took to be my spiritual self. It was the same procedure within myself at prayers. I would stand there among my class-mates four times a day, eyes closed, hands joined, knees pressed uncomfortably against the hard edge of the narrow, wooden desks, with that irascible face in front watching closely for any prankish gesture as we recited our prayers (boys who had been caned or slapped often took the opportunity to relieve their feelings by a stooping of the head, bringing the thumb of one joined hand to the nose, and cocking a snook). I would know I could not sincerely pray for one second in that odious place, with that teacher presiding, and uneasy and ashamed, and asking God's forgiveness for the deceit, I would join in a bogus, unfeeling chant: 'Bless us, O Lord, and these Thy gifts, which we are about to receive from Thy bounty, through Christ Our Lord, Amen.'

It was the common practice for each teacher to have the class cane displayed as a cautionary warning, usually supported on the pegs of the easel which held the blackboard, yet the teaching staff could not be said to be wholly responsible for the brooding air of oppression and chastisement that seemed to invade the entire building, and every corner of the school playground, through the narrow passage to the old, battered side-door in Houghton Street, which let one out into the free world once more, a release at the day's end which most boys greeted with some wild, impulsive whoop of delight. Among the senior teachers there was Mr Seddon, known to the boys as Jackie, a most reasonable man; also his youthful brother, Harold, who sported a clipped moustache; Mr Kelly, the golfer, was not a bad chap; then Mr Winstanley, known as P. Winney, a tall, earnest man with light, wavy hair; and even Mr J. V. Smith, the headmaster, was fair and impartial, though not given to clemency; and, of course, there had been my own gentle Miss Conway. But the spirit of the place was one of correction, and no one appeared to have the character or will to change it.

The most fearsome teacher in the school was Miss Brown, and although by chance I had a few months in her class, she and I had come to an understanding. Miss Brown—Veronica, I recall from her signature on the register was her first name—was the elder and more dominant of two sisters, both teachers, the younger one in the Infants' School. Veronica was a short, bantamweight lady, made up, it seemed, of bone, muscle and gristle, with scarcely enough flesh on any part of her body for one to pinch between two fingers, yet she didn't look thin, just hard. She had bony cheekbones, firmly sunken cheeks, a strong nose, fierce mouth with lips hidden, and eyes like two cold, gleaming buttons. Her scrawny neck, with its outsize Adam's apple, and her face and the upper bosom, were composed of the same leathery texture, a sallow brown with a dull lustre, as though the entire surface had been scrubbed with carbolic soap and left to dry in an east wind. She had little hair, or at least what she had was sparse, for its frizzy presence seemed but to accentuate the lines of a bullet-shaped skull. Her age was a mystery, and she might have passed as a youthful ninety, or an aged nineteen, since it seemed she had never been other than what she was now—as though she had been born with that hard little figure, knobbly face, and scant hair, and, impervious to time and all else, she would go into her wooden box exactly the same. It was not a face that would attract undue attention in Lancashire of the day, for there were other women of a similar mould, but they would mostly be seen working the outdoor hoists at cotton-waste factories or serving coal to youngsters at the coal-yard, but such an exceptionally tough face was unusual in the teaching profession.

Miss Brown appeared before the class each morning in an immaculately ironed blouse of crêpe de Chine, the freshness and femininity of which served only to highlight her uncomely features; no blouse, however, could survive the pulsations that went on in that breast, and by noon the starch would have collapsed, and the garment would be crumpled and moist. All that, it must be said, was more or less on the surface, and the shock came when Miss Brown opened her mouth. She suffered from, or perhaps enjoyed—since it in no way imparied her speech—a chronic huskiness, and her voice began its journey deep down in the lungs, forced its way up by the bronchi and trachea to the larynx, gathering depth and power along the way, and was finally expelled with a startling male gruffness, having gathered to itself tiny flecks of spittle which would cascade into the air, bedewing those in the front row of the classroom. Brave indeed was the boy who heard that curiously resonant croak and could detach himself from a sense of dread, a foreboding that something unpleasant was about to happen. The special, harsh rasp which she insinuated on occasion, slow and penetrating—the baleful prelude to a caning—served to produce in some boys a paralysed terror, perhaps in the way a snake is said to exert a like condition on a victim by its hiss. 'Mundy,' she would hoarsely coo the boy's surname, with a fearful relish, 'I'm going to scarify you!'

(Thirty years later I was to meet the same Mundy, now a notorious cat burglar, who had recently been let out of prision: 'Remember ol' Miss Brown,' he said, "ow she used threaten to *scallify* you? An' she bloody did—she did that an' all! But tha's got to admit, the same as Fat Ada, she wur a damn good teacher—tha knows wut I mean, she'd knock sense into thee, one way or t'other. Ee, but they gave me some bloody humpy they did when I were a lad.' An incident to do with the same Francis Mundy was told me by one chap I met on a visit to Bolton: 'I wur in this pub in Deane Road,' he told me, 'this Sat'day teatime, see, nearly empty it wur, when in come Francis, orders a pint, an' buys one for this mate of his, who wur sittin' theer lookin' glum, an' Francis says: "Wut's up—tha looks bloody miserable, Sam?" So Sam says: "Sunday tomorrow, Francis, an' I aren't been able to get 'um a roast or owt for t'Sund'y dinner. I wouldn't mind so much for me an' the wife, it's the kids we worry about. They allus look forward to summat to eat of a Sunday." So's Francis says, "Hang on a tick—I might be able t'elp thee out." Then he downs his pint an' goes off. It seems he's gone round to Steele's provision warehouse, just up the road, climbed a rain-spout, got in through a window, an' in about ten minutes he's back, orders two pints, opens his jacket, an' there underneath he has this lovely hunk of boilin' bacon, about ten pounds in weight. So he says to this mate of his: "Wut about that, Sam—will that do thee ant' wife ant' kids for tomorrow?" So's Sam looks at it, an' he says: "It's a right good piece, Francis, it is that an' all, a good weight, too, but would tha say it wur a bit on t'fat side?—me ant' wife wouldn't mind but kids don't like fat." So's Francis says: "Howd on to it, Sam—an' if kids want a lean 'un I'll go back an' get 'um one." So he sups his pint, an' goes off back to Steele's provision warehouse—up t'rain-spout an' in through a window, an' it seems he gets Sam a full ham this time, lean as could be. Leastways, that's wut he gets charged wi' on Monday mornin', for sum'dy musta tipped off the law, because when Francis gets down t'rain-spout there's these two 'tecs waitin' for him.")

Miss Brown would skilfully twirl the long cane under the boy's armpit, and, after the usual ineffectual resistance, induce him by threats to hold out his hand, a limp, half-curled, and trembling hand, then, as she raised the cane ready to bring it down—at the same time anticipating, mostly with acute judgement, whether or not he had in mind a notion to withdraw his hand at the last moment—she had a nifty foot movement which she would exercise, doing a half-turn, and striking the pose of a flamenco dancer as she brought the weight from one foot to another so as to get the full purchase, as it were, for swinging the cane down in one of her powerful swishing strokes. When the caning was finally over—four raps was the limit—Miss Brown would turn, face the class, and, retaining a grip on her cane, eye them all over, daring any boy to betray a rebellious hint, and ready to take on all comers. Then she had a curious habit of turning almost tenderly toward her victim, who was usually caught up in half-swallowed sobs, and moans, all of which she appeared to get a satisfaction from, and there would come over her face what seemed to be a look of squalid reconciliation, almost approaching pity. It was said that, after a year in Miss Brown's class, no boy was ever normal again. (At rare moments, I must admit, it seemed I got a glimpse of another Miss Brown inside the one I have told of, and although she had that same untender look, she was tingling with a fierce dedication to teach, or at least to knock a little elementary knowledge into the forty or so boys in her custody, whom she detested, and no matter how difficult or distasteful the task, she would never waver, slacken or give in, but would do her job and her duty in the only way she knew how, and if the heavens were to open and gentle angels descend to her side to guide her it would be of no avail, for Veronica Brown could only go the way she had to go, for better or for worse.

On Friday mornings, Miss Brown might enter the school playground with a determinedly neutral look—warmth of any kind being rather beyond her—and although her presence struck some chord of fear in the yelling mass of boys, causing an immediate wide path to be presented to her, she would look neither to right nor left, but gaze blindly ahead, as though to shut from sight any behaviour which would invite censure. And it was the same with Miss Newsham, she would have an almost amiable expression, suggesting she had had enough of scolding, caning, and the handing out of punishment for one week, and now hoped for one final harmonious day at the weekend with her pupils. Alas, these expectations were never to be gratified, for sooner or later some unfortunate lad was bound to slip up.

The violations of which one could be found guilty were so numerous that none of us could ever feel wholly innocent, and many boys developed a natural reaction of doing some wanton mischief, such as scratching a desk with a knife, damaging the bulbs growing in bowls on the windowsill—anything over which they could be sure they would not get caught, in an effort to get even for the unjust punishments they had had to take.

One cannot say what was the ultimate effect of all these chastenings, but I do know that three boys from my own class did spells at reformatory institutions and later in prison, and that Francis Mundy, a small and friendly boy, whose main distinction was that of walking around the playground and up the steps on his hands, feet in the air, spent much of his adult life in prison. (On looking back it is not a recriminatory feeling which rises in me so much as a sense of regret over a missed opportunity. Here we were, teachers and pupils, all belonging to the same Christian faith, a Catholic minority one, a faith supposed to be based on love, and intended to pervade all teaching, so there might have been created, with a little affection and understanding from the staff, something beyond the scope of the ordinary elementary school, that special feeling of a spiritual or religious fraternity, which would have fostered a spirit of learning, responsibility, and goodwill toward each other. Nor should it be imagined when, to this present day, I feel such keen nostalgic affection for all my old school-mates, have memories only of gratitude and respect toward our school church and its kindly priests—especially dear Canon Holmes —that I do not experience more than a twinge of compunction that I must write in the way I do about my Alma Mater.)

The almost endless caning and other punishment (such as holding a boy's head under the cold water tap and scrubbing it), which would normally begin the moment official school time was signalled every morning—appeared to stem in the first place from an irreconcilable discrepancy between the set hygienic demands made by the school authority, and the inability of certain boys from poor homes to meet these; also a curriculum designed to achieve standards of education of a level certain pupils were incapable of reaching—and any breach of either meriting reprimand. Standards had to be set, but most boys were dependent on their mothers for cleanliness and appearance, and for getting them off to school on time, and some unfortunate mothers seemed to have no idea of hygiene or punctuality. As for learning, many boys came from homes in which one or other parent was illiterate, some were not too sound in the head, and these homes were dingy, dark dwellings in which the adults, inured to generations of work that was menial and dirty, and sunk down as they were in poverty and ignorance from birth to death, had little of intellectual value to pass on to their offspring; they were creatures who avoided all contact with the world of education.

These homes would usually be without watch or clock of any sort (factory buzzers and frequent calls on neighbours or passers-by served to keep the family informed), so that a boy from such a home would have no idea of how to tell the time, and would have to endure caning and abuse over being taught to read the clock. Life itself being so grim a reality to such a one, he was wholly unprepared for abstraction, and no matter how he struggled, it seemed impossible for him to grasp what the English lesson was about. Indeed, the very idea that speech had rules which needed to be learnt came as a shock to most boys, as it did to me, for a simple and familiar instrument was suddenly made complex and remote. The letter *a* had now to be recognized as the *indefinite article*; such a complex definition of a single letter did not appear to make sense. There was the adjective—the word itself was intimidating. It was a part of speech which baffled many of these boys right up to the top class, and severe were the canings which ignorance of it resulted in. Some boys had difficulty with the verb, unless it was reduced to its simplest form: The player *kicked* the ball. Certain boys looked on grammar as a guessing-game, and felt uncertain over the noun, vague about the pronoun, and bewildered by the preposition. The English lesson poisoned any desire they may have had to learn their own language. (Nor did I escape a decided inhibition about actually getting down to the learning of English grammar. Even today I find myself relying upon a feel for idiom, allied to a lively concern for exactitude of expression, helped along by an amateurish affection and respect for the English language and some long, but light, acquaintance with Fowler. Also, it seems to me—although this may be an illusion—that a thought itself always appears to be grammatically pure.)

It was a regulation of SS Peter and Paul's that each boy had to be either present in the actual playground, or within a few seconds' running distance from it when the first whistle was blown by the headmaster at ten minutes to nine each weekday morning. The shrill peremptory toot of that whistle was a command for instant silence and immobility, so that within a second of its first note, what had been a mob of racing and yelling boys would be transformed into a hushed collection of stilled figures, each one mute and frozen into any peculiar attitude in which the whistle may have caught him. This pause would be held for some moments, and would be followed by a sharp whistle, the signal for all boys to speed off and line up in the playground in the place prescribed for each class. It was during this resurge of activity, which might allow up to ten seconds' of sorting out time, that dawdlers, tin-can footballers, marble or cigarette-card players, and odd groups and individuals who preferred to linger outside the playground, and from there had heard the whistle and the silence descend, as well as many genuine latecomers, would make a frenzied dash for the school-yard door, then a wild rush to the alleyway that led into the school playground. This narrow passage, leading to the haven of safety, would often get blocked by the disorderly ingress of the boys, for some might stumble and fall, brief fights could break out, and a jam might ensue in the wild scramble to get a foot in the actual playground before the third whistle blew, which whistle served as an order for lines to start marching round the yard, one after the other, in proper order, and then to step briskly into school. Any boy failing to join his class before it entered the school door was accounted a latecomer.

Hovering close to the exit from the passage into the playground would be one of Mr Smith's head monitors, some hefty boy of thirteen, or possibly fourteen, if his parents had decided he could stay on for an extra year's education. Such boys were always drawn from the best families, those on friendly terms with the rector and other priests, boys who in most cases would serve as altar boys, and could almost be assured of going through their entire school life without a caning. This guardian would then set his back against one side of the passageway wall, and, choosing an appropriate moment, would thrust his leg up against the other wall, effectively barring the way. Threats, or bribes of toffee or even money, availed nothing against such characters, for they were already powerful little men, well-fed, vested in authority, against whom the menaces and fulminations of the toughest ordinary boy were so much bluster.

On certain mornings, perhaps once or twice a week, the entire boys' senior school—ages seven to thirteen—would be kept in class lines in the playground, for what was known as 'hygiene inspection'. The demands, modest enough, were that each boy be well washed, especially round the neck and inside his ears, that his hair be clean and brushed or combed into place, that hands be clean, nails scrubbed and unbitten, that he be clean and tidy in dress, wearing either a collar or jersey—scarves not permitted—that his stockings did not hang down, and that his clogs or boots were clean and polished. Mercifully, the most obnoxious offence against hygiene, was one which passed unmentioned—being that of the unfortunate boy from a poor home who gave off a bad odour. Almost the worst discomfort that could happen to me was to be placed next to such a boy in class. I had involuntary reactions to such, and whilst I was feeling an intense nausea, I would attempt to put on a chummy air to avoid hurting the boy's feelings. I believe that, apart from a lack of personal washing and clean underclothes, it had much to do with living in a bug-infested house, for from such homes there was a verminous stench which seemed to attach itself to the person and his clothes. And one or two I recall were intelligent boys, but woefully withdrawn. For them there was, apart from Flash Street clinic—a visit to which would invite discredit if not odium—no agency or group concerned with or sympathetic to their plight; and there seemed no understanding of how the child himself was helpless. Indeed, such children, although they might excite a swift, cold pity, tended to repel compassion, for a smelly child, infested with nits and lice—hair closely cropped, whether boy or girl, a state which shamed the child —and probably exhibiting the unsightly circular patches of ringworm, was not an object on which it was easy to exercise tenderness, since disgust so often intervened, nor was the cringing character such visitations produced likely to endear. Even amongst the good-hearted Lancashire people they became social lepers of a sort. (An unfortunate after-effect of being brought up in a home where there needed to be a constant destroying of vermin was a sort of phobia—I did not myself escape it—a state in which the first impulse toward any insect, from the bee to the harmless ladybird, was instantly to kill.)

There were certain boys from well-ordered homes who could fulfil all the school demands for cleanliness without a care, but they were in a minority, and there was a larger middle group that might be classed as dubious, and then there was also a bunch that might mistakenly be classed as incorrigible when in fact they were doomed, for there was no way they could escape. The working-class schoolboy such as myself (the fortunate one that is, from a relatively good home), usually possessed two shirts in all—one on and one in the wash—and after his weekly top-and-tailer at the kitchen sink, he put on his clean shirt on Saturday evening, or more likely Sunday morning for Mass, and then he wore it all the week, and slept in it every night. Indeed he hardly ever took it off except at weekends, and after a few days it was inclined to become grubby and sweat-stiffened. This stale condition did not impose itself on the wearer in the way that may be imagined, since it was the custom, and customs were not questioned. Pyjamas were almost unknown amongst the working class (they might be bought for going away at holiday time, but otherwise remain unworn); also, in winter the stone-floored homes were so cold that changing into a sleeping garment at night was an uninviting prospect. Even a good wash seemed to keep one awake.

But back to school life; in my own case the daily difficulties were increased by the collar I wore, a broad, respectable, celluloid one, fashioned on the Eton collar, which held the neck in grip; it required a collar-stud, and studs were the most elusive items. Many scenes of panic took place when I was on the last minute for school and my collar-stud could not be found. But I was one of the fortunate ones, for most of the boys could not afford such a collar, which cost one-and-sixpence, and the first blow in a fight could tear off one of the tabs held by the stud. These boys, or rather their mothers, would adopt sartorial stratagems, such as one which gave the appearance of a wool jersey, which for a long time I envied, until I discovered that it was only a jersey front, about one square foot, attached to the braces by loops. This device served well, except that it developed in the wearer a furtive reflex action, in which he kept pushing the front inwards to avoid discovery. The boys who were ill-dressed, with dirty clogs and unwashed ears, were usually those from homes where there was no clock, and so would often be amongst the latecomers, ordered to stand in the alleyway until

Mr Smith arrived with his special long cane. 'No clock—that excuse won't do—out with your hand.'

Certain boys used a dodge of withdrawing the hand as the cane came down, but this set going the headmaster's temper, whilst others would howl with pain and hop around on their toes, and some boys would let out long winces. My own response was based on a notion of not giving up my sense of personal dignity, no matter what happened, and if it was a cold day, when the cane caused the spurt of pain to run up the arm, I would set my teeth and lips tight, making out to the head master, as I did to Miss Newsham, that I was above it all. Possibly it was that attitude which caused me to remember it all so clearly. Very often the latecomer, when he reached his own classroom, would have his punishment endorsed by a period of kneeling upright behind the classroom door. This always struck me as a particularly humiliating punishment, with the monitors and others moving in and out of the classrooms. However, when I was ordered to do it, in Miss Newsham's class, I found some comforting solitude in being set apart, and I started praying in earnest—mental prayers, of course—mostly with some fierce resolve to get even with her (which, possibly, I am indulging in as I write—and if so, may God forgive me).

This harsh form of school life, which became centred to such a degree round transgression on one side and retribution on the other, appeared to crush out all other sensibility and inhibit any other form of relationship or understanding between teacher and pupil. The impact on me, as on so many boys, was one of shock, which had to be concealed; I felt guilty, unhappy, and uneasy—even though I could escape most punishments that came to those unfortunate boys who were less brainy. My feeling was that such teachers as Miss Brown and Miss Newsham belonged to another world, a brutal and mad one. Largely I submitted, resigning myself to established authority that was stronger than my own power to resist.

But it was a near thing. I never went beyond a form of dumb insolence—I would look at the teacher, accept my caning, and hope that the thoughts behind my impassive look would communicate themselves. But on occasion I came near to rebelling. It wasn't lack of courage held me back, but the feeling that I would have to cast aside so much else if I once made the move.

This stern emphasis on discipline, which was tied to that of retribution and sin, seemed to be a basic flaw in Catholic education. In the 'penny' catechism, which every Catholic child had to 'know by heart', each of the twelve articles of the Apostles' Creed was examined, and the tenth article, 'the forgiveness of sins', took up eighteen questions and answers. Of these, only two made a passing reference to this divine compassion and liberation of forgiveness, the other sixteen concentrated on original sin and actual sin, venial sin and mortal sin—'Where will they go who die in mortal sin?' 'They who die in mortal sin will go to hell for all eternity.' Such teaching so coloured the child's attitude to God and himself that he was lumbered with inhibitions and his orientation tended not to the good life so much as to avoidance of sin. It was painfully clear why one must fear God, but there seemed no reason for loving Him. I feel sure that, had I been taught of 'the God within', I should have had a happier and richer sense of life—and of both God and myself.

# 17

Death, non-existence, is a state I often consider, and would enjoy talking about with others, but I can never find another eager to share in such a conversation; and it is the same with old age, most people prefer to avoid mentioning it, and when I insist that the changes come so unexpectedly, that no matter how much one has seen, one has never truly realized what old age is, I often get the reply, 'You are only as old as you feel—you are not old.' The fact is, I feel not only old but find it natural to do so, and am unenvious of those who insist they are still young—which is something I have never heard a young person mention. Indeed, I don't think I have ever felt young since the age of seven. I remember when I was nine a boy call Ernie Selby from the street-corner died. 'What a pity,' I heard someone say, 'just when he had turned fourteen and could have gone working full-time.' Others said it was a shame to go so young. But I thought it over seriously in bed, and decided that if I lived another five years—an incredibly long period—I should be fairly satisfied; fourteen is a fair age, I thought. Recently I found myself replying to someone who said I wasn't old: 'If you remember seeing German Zeppelins over Bolton in the First World War, and you've walked through the streets next morning where they dropped their bombs, you're old—no matter what anyone tells you!' It may be that there is an aura of age about me, for one day when I was in my fifties, watching a football match, a Chelsea pensioner gave me a nudge: 'Dad,' he said, 'you 'aven't got a match, 'ave you?' To be called 'Dad' by a Chelsea pensioner flattered me greatly and I went off to borrow matches for him.

I doubt if I ever saw an actual Zeppelin, but many people said they did, and my brother Edward declares that on the moonlight night they bombed Bolton, he looked out of our back-bedroom window and saw the Zeppelin, the crew moving around inside, and the bombs being dropped out of the airship; but Edward has been known to stretch things a bit. What you could see on dark winter evenings during the Great War, when you were standing at the street-corner with your mates, was the flashing of numerous searchlights in the dark sky overhead; you didn't see the actual beam but the white oval space it illuminated in the sky, and the impression I got was of huge, white shapes, not unlike some horrible fish, darting about in the sky above. Some boy would cry out: 'A Zepp!—did ya see it!—over theer—nar, not theer—by gum, he's turned round an' gon t'other way!' The Zeppelins came after midnight mostly, perhaps on two or three occasions, and although I probably never saw one I talked as if I had. On 11 November 1918—the eleventh hour of the eleventh day of the eleventh month, as they were so fond of pointing out to us—the Armistice was signed, and the Great War was over. I remember that came to me as an infinite relief, and with it went a half-day off school.

The expression 'The War' had been in the air for four years, and had been bandied about so much that I had come to feel 'The War' was literally in the atmosphere. When I stood at the street-corner in the evening, with the almost incessant fog glistening greyishly under the corner lamp, I took all this dark, dank stuff to be part of 'The War', and that as soon as that was over, it too would come to an end. There was a great change, and for a start it seemed the weather improved, right on to the wonderful summer of 1921. Among the people there was—as I now recall it—a feeling of some kind of shock. The actual war casualties, bad as they were, were fewer around us than may be thought, since most industrial workers could not be spared from cotton, coal, and munitions jobs, and a high proportion of those outside these occupations who volunteered or were called up were C3 and unfit for military service; poverty, ignorance, and bad conditions having sorely affected the physical condition of the people. There were few streets, however, in which a mother had not lost a son, or the home a father, and men with a limb or two missing were common around the town. Standing at the edge of the group at the Men's Corner I noticed that the chaps who had served in India would talk of life there, and even those who had been to Mesopotamia and still showed signs of malaria would talk of marching through the desert, but with the odd exception there seemed a tacit agreement amongst those who had been in the trenches to keep silent about France, as though the experience had been too hideous or shameful to be told at a street-corner. Right after the war the next affliction was known as 'The Flu,' and none of us escaped it except Uncle William, although even the flu couldn't get him, for he was, as the Irish have it, as healthy as a stone.

The misery and suffering of the poorer people in those days—we were relatively prosperous at the time—when pain-relieving and sleeping drugs were almost unknown, and whisky was beyond the purse, can scarcely be imagined. The post-war influenza epidemic was a virulent one, and it seemed that almost everybody was suffering from its effects, with aches in the limbs, pains across the back, sick headaches, inflammation, and a general sense of weakness so total that all there could be ahead seemed to be death itself. And of course there were many deaths. Conversely, there was the bright side, for those who have suffered a sickness through without any real alleviation, experience a beautiful switch to normal feeling once the body starts recovering, and the relief almost compensates for all the sick and racking weariness. The sharing of this kind of suffering drew people together in some curious way, and man and wife who were at daggers drawn normally, would learn to sympathize with and understand the other, when there was a malady common to both.

Uncle William was still a dataller down the mine—my father had got better-paid work at the coal-face—but Uncle seldom missed a turn's work, doing the six shifts a week that was expected of the men, especially during the War. Nearby Uncle William's lodgings in Chequerbent there was a farm, and all through the war years of labour shortage he would help the farmer, working a couple of hours daily in the afternoon, and in summer months he worked until late in the evening at the haymaking after having done his morning shift at the mine. He seemed to be a contented man, for he both liked and respected the English, and particularly the Lancashire English of the day, who were mostly hard-working and houseproud. A good handyman in those days, one who could repair a broken window-cord or make a plant-pot stand for the aspidistra, was said to be able to 'tron,' and, surprisingly for an Irishman, Uncle William was a good 'tron' or 'tronner,' to which activity he brought his own artistic touch.

I recall a weekday morning around 1916, when he and I were together in the back kitchen of our little home in Bolton, and

Mother brought us in tea and soda cake, and there was the peaceful atmosphere that always sprang up when my father, who was doing a week on day shift, was absent. Uncle William was wearing bellbottom trousers supported by broad braces and a good leather belt—he always bought the best—and the sleeves of his thick flannel shirt were rolled up, showing sturdy arms. Next he put on a large, coarse apron—known in Bolton as 'a brat'—which he had brought with him. All the time he went about with a gentle smile on his face, for although at times firm and even stubborn, he was seldom ill-humoured, cross or contrary. He had brought the table in from the front kitchen, spread newspapers on it, and on these he now upturned three small canvas bags and out poured broken delft, a bright mass of coloured bits of porcelain, fragments of willow pattern plates, bits of china cups and saucers, and broken eggcups. I began to rummage amongst the piles, but he gently discouraged me, for he was like a man who wanted to get his eye in, as it were, and needed some calm and quiet. On the table he placed two large, circular tins, each a foot in diameter, with raised sides round the circumference edge—which had tiny bits of Cleeve's Limerick toffee encrusted on the sides, which I scraped off and ate. He also had a bag of plaster of Paris, and, after making a very good job of scouring the tins, Uncle mixed the plaster of Paris very carefully, then lined the inside of one tin with the paste, and next set it almost upright, where it would catch the light from the back window. Then he spread the coloured bits of china and porcelain over the table and began his task.

He stood back from the table, and then he selected one of the pieces of broken delft, a brightly-coloured piece, and after a moment's hesitation set it at the spot he fancied in the circle of grey paste. Then he took up another piece and placed it beside it, and he began to get into the mood, it seemed, blending the bits of pottery as his fancy prompted, working briskly but unhurriedly, and doing it all in a manner not unlike that of an artist with a picture, continually stepping back and turning his head a little to one side as he judged the effect, and humming a tune to himself, as was his habit. Naturally enough, I wanted to join in, and was more than a little put out when the most I could get out of him was to be allowed to choose a single piece, and then he held my hand and placed the piece in the spot he thought best—but even at that I could see he wasn't entirely pleased, and would probably have not chosen that piece at all. I wearied of watching him and, since he was disinclined to talk, took myself off into the street, for I felt it all to be a bit daft for a grown-up man to be sticking bits of broken pottery onto a toffee tin. When I got back home I found he had finished the first plaque. It was a mosaic, created by a simple arrangement of broken china and delft, with the odd piece of purple glass, and in the centre was the half of a broken eggcup, placed in such a way that there was a handy upright cavity. Uncle William finished off the pair of plaques, attached hooks and cords, and finally hung them from the picture-rail that was in the front kitchen.

I remember they hung there for many years, and as is the case in such small homes, they seemed to become part of the fixtures, as immovable as the oven itself. They were much admired, although I got a feeling that my father was restrained in expressing his opinion of them as pictures on a wall. I remember the eggcup proved a handy place for Mother to hide the odd sixpence or two on a Friday, when money was around, and then during the week, if I was cadging threepence to go to the pictures she would say: 'Maybe I have something in Uncle's eggcup.' Although I was crafty I could rarely bring myself to put prying fingers into that eggcup, unless I was desperate, but when I was that way I would do almost anything.

Uncle William lodged in Chequerbent with a respectable family by the name of Bellis. He greatly enjoyed his part-time work at the farm, was a natural worker, and on my visits there I was struck by how they were always calling out 'Billy!', for he was much in demand. Certain Saturday mornings he would borrow the farmer's horse-and-cart and drive to the pit to pick up the load of coal every miner was allowed to buy at a cheaper rate, bring it in to us, tip it at our back gate, and join in helping to stack it in the coal-shed in the backyard. Then I would climb into the cart beside him and go back to the farm with him, some four miles away. He would do an hour or two of work round the farm, showing me off at the same time, and then we'd go into Bellis's. He would drink tea and get himself ready to return with me for the evening.

From being a barefoot lad around the roads of Tubber, Uncle William had become, in his fifties, a man of some substance in his own simple way. He was a bachelor, in a day when a bachelor was accorded some extra touch of respect—the celibate life being regarded as morally above the married state, at least among Irish Catholics (at home in Ireland he had been nicknamed William the Priest). He fitted well into the role of bachelor, with his avuncular warmth and generosity. He valued respectablity, and doing the decent thing in every situation. His natural self-esteem was perhaps given more substance, if this is not too crude a way to put it, by owning two or three pairs of good boots and two suits; he always kept a pound or two in the pocket, so that there was no company in which he could not hold his own. That was the one thing that counted—for a man to be able to hold his own. Besides the money in his pocket he had a handy sum put away, so he need refuse no friend who came to borrow as many did. He had a good name wherever he went. He could enter any public-house, any home, any company, no one could say a word against him, and he could look any man in the face—not that he would be so rude. But, as much as he was drawn to the English and English ways, at the heel of the hunt he was Irish, and at times proud of it, although modestly so. He allowed himself to get drunk occasionally, but such lapses were mostly forced upon him by company—for, truth to tell, he was by nature inclined to be temperate; and anyway, taking the odd glass too many was said to be a good man's fault, and although somewhat ashamed of himself later, if he did no worse he wouldn't do too badly. A man had to let others see that he was just as normal as they were, and could take on the open and unguarded periods of one not sober. He attended Mass every Sunday and took the sacrament once or twice a year—not too often, that would look as though one had something on one's conscience—and he kept to his work, but again took the odd day off to show he was not without an easy-going streak, just like the next man, and thanks be to God he not only had his job, but his good health.

There was this certain split taking place in my favoured relationship with my Uncle William over those later war years. I had sensed at once when we landed in England that I was his favourite, and I played on this, so that I had a particular self set aside for Uncle William, one that I had taken up rather to please and flatter him—apart from the occasion when he attempted to carry me to school—and one that as I grew older I found more difficult to sustain. Yet I could see no way of shedding it and starting all again on a natural basis. This may happen in relationships in which one person is loved by another, but does not feel a corresponding sense of true love (and when I analyse my then feelings about Uncle William it is not real love I find, but a need to be in with someone of influence), yet there is the attraction of those benefits the person provides—and Uncle William did make a wonderful difference to our home life, and above all to Mother—in which the person himself is mislaid.

There was another incident in those early years in Bolton which stuck in my mind, and left me less well-inclined to Uncle William. It took place one Sunday morning after he had stayed the night with us, having planned to take us children, including baby James, to have our photograph taken along with him at Willis's studio on Bradshawgate to send home to Ireland. Sunday mornings were not happy occasions, because in the home where there is drinking, the evenings may be jolly enough, but not so the mornings after, and we as children got used to that cycle of varying home atmosphere, the rise and fall of which were related to drink and the things that go with it. An accustomed smell in the home on such mornings was that given off by stale beer left clinging to unwashed glasses from the evening before. Just as fresh beer seemed to have a pleasant and promising smell in the evening, so the unsavoury odour of stale beer appeared to carry squalid echoes next morning of foolish things done, said, and thought the evening before, and there were hints of the unreality of the evening's joviality when its traces were exposed to the clear, cold light of day.

In my father's case the disillusion he exposed was not solely from the bad head and depression, which were misfortune enough, but would emerge on discovering he had less money in his pocket than he had imagined. He would then go over what he had spent the night before, and come to the conclusion that he had been too decent in paying, and others had not been decent enough. I was well aware that in his morning silence lurked the embers of ill-temper that would spring into flame if fanned at all. Fortunately, Mother was not given to drink, and although she would take a glass of stout or even a taste of whiskey, she would do it for the sake of the company, and I never saw her take even a sip when there were not people pressing her to do so. An overriding element was that she scarcely ever did anything purely for herself. The simplest of things pleased her, such as a nice cup of hot, fresh tea with a taste of buttered potato cake. If she were allowed to eat that for once in peace, without jumping up and down from the table, she looked upon it as a luxury.

On Sunday mornings my father chose to get up first, as Saturday was the one night the fire did not require banking up, and so it could be allowed to go out. He would make a big job of removing all the ashes and cleaning under the oven, in order that the fire, which he would then light, would draw sufficiently to heat the oven for the cooking of the Sunday dinner. He was a fearsome figure at such times, clomping around the house in his old boots, wearing a singlet and old trousers, with a look of bleary ill-temper set on his face, almost like an animal ready to pounce, in the way one ill-chosen remark would set him off. He would be bearing the shovelfuls of ashes through the back kitchen and out into the backyard to be put into the ashtub in what was called the midden, his mouth pulled into some sort of a savage grimace, in an effort to threaten the wind and the elements in case they should attempt to blow the ashes off the shovel. 'That bloody Magee's beer has my head split,' he would say when he was well enough to speak at all, 'sure it's nothin' but flamin' chemic'. Keep outa my way willya now!'

It sometimes happened that Uncle William would miss the last tram back to Four Lane Ends, and then he would stay the night. I remember one occasion when both Uncle William and Uncle Mick stayed at our house, and I was put sleeping in the back bedroom with them. I had gone up to bed earlier, but was wide awake, in the inside place next to the wall. The two men chatted quietly as they undressed and each put his clothes on the chairs that Mother had provided. Then each in his flannel shirt, knelt beside the bed to say prayers. They spoke them softly and clearly, the Our Father, Hail Mary, and Glory be, after which they made a special prayer for a happy death. Uncle William, I remember, would always make a special thing of that prayer—and a happy death implicitly meant to die in Ireland.

When Uncle William stayed the night, he would appear next morning with his usual gracious manner, no sign of a bad head on him, but his quiet smile, as though half asking was there anything anyone needed. You could stand there and chat to him as he was shaving—having borrowed my father's hollow-ground razor, which I felt was lent him with reluctance cloaked in flummery: 'I have that sharpened to a great edge now, William, so go careful with it for fear you'd cut yourself.' It is an odd thing, I used to think, how someone given to unpleasant moods will so easily put them aside when there is another there whose presence either intimidates or casts a gentle glow. 'That's the finest razor you ever put to your face—the Germans made it—sure they talk of their Sheffield steel but the bloody Germans are the lads when it comes to makin' a razor.' And then he would look round for someone he could cast his look on, so as to give weight to his words, and sure enough it would have to be me. No matter what may have been said against me, no one could say I was not prepared to listen.

On this certain Sunday morning when I was six years old, there was the question, amongst others, as to how I should be bathed, so as to be clean and shining for my photograph to be taken. Uncle William said he would give me a bath, and that I should stand up naked on the slopstone. He would give me a wash down from a bowl of warm water and then a cold rinse, so that I would be spotless. I didn't want him to, because Mother was the only one I liked around me at a time like that—or perhaps another woman, but certainly not a man. I agreed, for it was hard to disagree with Uncle William, and he had promised me sixpence, and also, in such a small house with so many people around me and so much going on, it seemed that one often got involved and carried along before one had quite time to think things out and refuse. Finally I undressed and crouched naked, shivering away on the cold slopstone, trying to hide my private parts and attempting not to look embarrassed, and putting one foot after the other in a bowl of soapy water that was set down on the slopstone and was too hot, so I'd have to pull a foot out and then feel the cold stone on the soles of my feet, and, as bad as it all was, I kept making out it was even worse.

Uncle William was wearing an apron, and he took up the scrubbing brush, and put soap on it and began to scrub my legs. I let out a howl, for the pain the coarse fibres brought to my skin was unbelievable. Mother stood nearby trying to placate me with looks and sighs. It was the old problem that had plagued me almost from birth—how it was that people using face flannels, brushes, and other things on you never seemed to realize how sensitive human skin is. I became aware that I would have earned my sixpence by the time he had done. He was persuaded by Mother to use the flannel, but his hands were hard, and he was quite ignorant of all my tender spots—at the top of the left ear, the end of my nose, my cheekbones, and above all the way that carbarbolic soap seemed to burn the eyes out of me if one wasn't careful. However, with sore nose, blinded eyes, stinging ear and other inflictions, I stuck it out, for sixpence was a lot of money, and by nature I was not disagreeable, and also I liked the idea of being clean. When the actual washing was at an end and I was covered with frothy soap, Uncle William took up the large, brown enamel jug, one that held almost a gallon, and filled it at the cold tap, whilst I snivelled, and tried to get a look in at Mother. Now he told me to hold my breath: 'This will do you all the good in the world,' he said. I watched him raise the jug over my head, I crouched expectantly, and the next thing he poured all the icy-cold water down over my naked body.

I was prepared for a feeling like that which I got when I washed at the slopstone and splashed my chest with water—a quick cold sensation followed by a nice tingling. I had no idea what it felt like to have a quart or two of cold water poured down my back and chest whilst standing on a slopstone in a cold back kitchen. The first sensation was of shock, blindness, breathlessness, with my lungs and chest paralysed, a form of cold, sharp death. I tried to let out a yell of 'Bloody hell!' but there was no wind in me, no nothing, it was like some horrible nightmare in which I was curled up helplessly. And it seemed as though, by some cruel magic, Uncle William had got hundreds of gallons into that one enamel jug, and it was running all down my back and would never cease. At last came the first gulp of breath—and like a new-born baby I let out a mad scream, and cried for Mother. She hurried to me, and, as wet as I was, I let myself fall straight into her arms, sobbing breathlessly. Nobody, except perhaps the mother, has the least true notion of what a sudden shock can do to a child (and here I am, almost seventy years later, writing of it as though it were this morning, it is still so vivid). At first I even refused Uncle William's sixpence, and had to be pressed hard to accept it.

Recently the photograph we had taken that day was sent to me from Ireland. I laughed a bit to see the group, but it gave me an odd cut at the heart. I saw myself seated there on a stool at the front of the group, wearing a jersey, chest out and shoulders back, and I recalled the spirited young chap I was, or had been—and how from then on life seemed to set about taming me. The wild spirit was well curbed by the time I left school at the age of fourteen. I find it returning now I am in my seventies.

# 18

It is Wednesday, the day before Christmas Day, 1919, and our front kitchen seems oddly grey and chilly, as Mother has had to let the coal-fire die down, so that she can blacklead and polish the range, all in preparation for the evening's festivity. The atmosphere of the home is dependent on the fire, and no home—except the most poverty-stricken one—is without a fire, even on the hottest day in summer. I am seated on a chair over near the window, a cheerless spot to be, but I prefer not to sit near my father, who is set up on his rocking-chair on the right of the fireside, reading the newspaper. He regards the presence of all children, especially his own, as a nuisance, which is one reason why I like to keep out of his way as much as I can. Not that we expect the personal interest or light joking manner, so touching in certain English fathers, since we know that the Irish father sees himself as the undisputed boss of all under his roof, but even so, no Irish father we know is so grumpy, and I wonder did his father treat him just as he treats us? Yet sometimes, when he is going off to pit in the evening, so quiet and sombre in his old pit clothes and heavy clogs, saddled with snapcan and big tea-can, and I go over to kiss him goodnight, and I see how pale and taut he is, compared with the big, loud, and open man he was back in Ireland, I get the odd twinge of uneasiness that I should have no real sympathy for my own father. And I understand how Mother allows his outbursts of temper to simply die out, seems to let pass his rancorous manner when he has drink taken, and is most sensitively concerned about his welfare in every way.

He looks over his newspaper now and again to watch her, with the sleeves of her blouse rolled up, gripping the blacklead brush in her small hands, the beads of sweat on her forehead, as she hums some jig in time with her polishing. 'Sure I don't mind how little you do,' she will say to my sister May when she does a job around the house, 'but for the Lord's sake put a bit of style in it. Och, America is the place where you'd see them workin' away in style.' She might give the odd extra spurt in attempting to raise a glow on the sulky iron of the oven and hob, which causes my father to look at her as though she were engaged in some activity that made little sense to him. She is behind with her housework, but this is more or less how it has to be, for she dare not risk having anything finished too early, since the soot, ash or a loose cinder could spoil the finished job.

The day has gone for her as follows: the knocker's-up call, a sort of tattoo with a whisk of wires at the end of a long pole, sounded on the front upstairs-window in the early morning: 'Quarther–past five, missis, quarther–past five!' he calls in a rather mournful voice. 'Thank you, sir!—thank you, sir!' she calls back. (Once, when I felt myself to be getting rather smart, I remarked that in Bolton you didn't call the knocker-up 'sir', and her reply to me was, 'that's exactly the man you do call "sir".' And she gave me a look of reproach that she should have to explain a thing like that to her own son.)

Mother gets out of bed, already whispering her morning prayers as she puts on a few clothes and hurries downstairs to tend the raked-up fire, to give the final stirring to the porridge in the big, iron pot that has stood slowly cooking on the hob beside the fire all night, then call my Cousin Willie, shake out his pit clothes which have been warming beside the oven to make sure there are no cockroaches in them, and prepare his breakfast. She says the odd prayer as she goes round the house, since she has only moments to spare to go down on her knees and take a comforting clasp of her rosary beads. Willie comes quietly down in undervest and long, wool pants, after saying his own prayers by the side of his bed, and dresses himself modestly in the back kitchen, calling out a greeting to Mother, and taking up his pit clothes which she has arranged for him on a chair. Over tea, Mother and Willie talk in their soft intimate whispers, and so good-humoured are the pair of them even at that early hour that seldom a morning passes without a laugh and joke.

Sometimes, as I am not a good sleeper, and am also curious, I go down to join them, and I can't think what it is they find funny at such an early hour. Often it is a mention of Ireland —what would they think of anyone over there who was up at a quarter–past five in the morning! And sometimes Mother is actually telling Willie about her dreams, and who in Ireland it was she dreamt of, all in a way she could never tell my father.

Then the sound of the swift *clop-clop* of Jimmy Schofield's pit clogs along the street signals that it is time Willie was off, and she hands him his snapcan, which he fastens to his belt, and also his huge tea-can, which he carries, and so, smiling nervously, wetting his lips with his tongue, and blessing himself, he bids goodbye, and with a shower of whispered 'Godspeeds!' and 'Go carefuls!' Mother goes to the door and sees him off in the dark, morning street. So close is this dear nephew to her that in some way he is nearer than a son—she is so concerned and protective over him. (When I recall the scene there seems almost a saintliness in the way Cousin Willie goes off to the hard, strange work down the pit with a quiet smile on his face.)

I got a fright one morning when I chanced to be downstairs in the front kitchen around half–past six and Mother was out in the backyard. Suddenly the front door opened, and in came a total stranger. I almost collapsed with shock at the sight of him. He looked fearsome, deformed, with the sign of a hump of sorts on his chest, and another near the bottom of his long jacket behind him. But far more frightening as he advanced towards me was his utter blackness—his face so black that it could have been rubbed with soot until not a speck of skin showed through. And set in that black face of the stranger in our home was a pair of gleaming eyes. I felt I ought to scream out for my mother, but my tongue had gone dry, and speech seemed beyond me. We stared at each other for a moment, and I thought my last day had come. What made it even worse was that in spite of his grotesque appearance there was something familiar about him, and it struck me he must surely be satan since he was said to come in a shape one would know. A mixture of feelings kept me from making some outburst—the dry mouth, even an ingrained sense of courtesy towards a stranger under our roof, and an Irish training from birth which dictated that one must never hastily ask for explanations of any kind, since all will be revealed in time if one only waits.

'Well, Willyeen,' said the stranger, 'what're ye doin' up at this hour!' And suddenly Mother was in the room, full of apology for not being there to greet him, and it seemed by magic she had a mug of tea in her hand, offering it to him. She took the hump from the rear of him which proved to be a huge, enamel tea-can, and he removed the bulge from his shirt which was a snapcan, and as I slowly recognized his voice, I made a bewildered realization that it was my own father. Well, I nearly made an eejit of myself then, I thought. In reply to her suggestion that he rest a minute or two, he said no, he wouldn't sit down, for if he did he'd never get up out of the chair, and if she had his hot water ready, he would wash and change at once. And so Mother hurried to pick up the iron pan of water from the hob and went into the back kitchen where she poured it into the big, enamel washbowl that stood on the slopstone.

Often it would later come out that my father had suffered some minor injury, as happened often among coal-miners, such as a strained back, a twisted ankle, or a knock from falling coal, but he would never mention such until later. Nor would my mother remark directly if she spotted something was wrong—a tough, silent front had to be adopted. But it would all come out later when he was rested; she might, however, casually mention something that was close, such as, 'Sure these clogs are a terrible weight.' This seemingly detached remark would some-how touch on an understanding or sympathy without bringing the thing itself into the open. With a weary coal-miner coming in from work the wife needed to be subtle. In addition to the common misfortunes of accidents at work, of bad housing, insufficient sleep, inadequate diet, and the host of illnesses from rheumatism to influenza that were part of the life, it seemed that each one had his own complaint; Willie suffered from migraine; Mother had broad feet, could never find shoes wide enough to fit her, and in consequence had corns and ingrowing toenails; my father was subject to boils.

On this particular morning Mother would have gone back to bed after Cousin Willie had gone off to work, to rest and maybe sleep for half an hour. Then she would be up again around half–past six so that all would be ready to greet my father when he got home from the night shift. He didn't like to see any of us around when he arrived—and we couldn't go downstairs whilst he was washing in the back kitchen, for he was modest and shy. Mother had to fit in the various comings and goings of everyone so that things could run smoothly. Next she had to have the three of us, Edward, May, and myself, up for breakfast, washed, dressed, and comforted—no school the day before Christmas, and to see that James the baby was looked after. She would than make the bed for my father, and let the other beds air. He would go off to bed around nine o'clock in the morning, and now she had to work briskly to get all the outside cleaning done, the front doorstep and the windowsill mopped and stoned, and do her best with the back kitchen and the mopping of the floor, leaving the finishing touches until later. Above all she had to make sure there was little noise, for my father was a light sleeper and the least sound could wake him and spoil his rest. In between she would hurry out and do her Christmas shopping and, above all, she must strive to keep everyone in a good mood, by finding each one some little job to do, and exercising her kind understanding, all spiced with humour, abundant hugging and kissing, maybe a quiet song or story thrown in, and, if needed, the odd touch of firmness.

We're through to late afternoon. May has gone next door to play with Alice, who is a half-timer in the mill, and has worked in the morning and is on holiday in the afternoon. Edward has gone off to visit his pal, Arthur Nixon, who was delicate—the common euphemism for consumption. James, the youngest, is sleeping in his cradle. I am reading *Kitchener's Army*—a large war-recruiting propaganda book, with hard, blue cover, which was given away free by our grocer, Edward Heyes Ltd, of Derby Street, around 1916.

My father seems put out at anyone reading when he is around: 'He won't have a steam of sight left in his two eyes, God save us, with the ould book stuck up to his nose readin'—when he should be out gettin' God's fresh air.' It hardly seemed God's fresh air in a place where you could not walk a few yards without getting a sooty speck in your eye. Maybe the poor man only wanted me out of the way so that he could relax. 'Well, surely it's little enough harm the poor ladeen will do if he never does more than read an innocent book,' says my mother. A remark like that is enough to bring up a sob of self-pity in my throat, and I do wish she would keep quiet. *Kitchener's Army* is considered better than comics, and largely escapes censure. There are pictures of new recruits, young and happy soldiers at their training camps, getting ready to go over to France. They look such a cheerful lot that I have often envied them, and wished I was with them. It is the only book in the home, and as I have a mania for reading, I have read it through so often and studied the pictures so long, that I know every soldier's face in it, and I know where they crop up in other pictures, and I have made many favourites amongst them, and also one or two I would avoid, for the face tells me everything.

'Sure isn't the world in a terrible way altogether?' remarks my father, pulling the newspaper down from in front of his face, and at the same time bringing forward his rocking-chair so that he can reach out for the mug of tea keeping warm on top of the oven. Mother is too much behind with her work to risk looking up and catching his eye, but I have heard him and am trying to put on an air of interest in something going on out in the street, just to avoid giving him a look of response. I don't know how to handle the kind of look my father gives, for I feel that if the devil himself were to come up out of hell and stand before me, at least some look of comprehension would pass between us, but with my father, no. Nothing except an awareness of discord. (One day, maybe some forty years ahead, there will be a genuine affection and understanding between us—but there is none of either now.)

I half turn to him, however, and am caught by his fierce stare. Before he speaks he always put on this look—or it comes in spite of himself—and holds it there without a word for as long as five seconds. I suppose in a way it is like an actor giving a cue to an audience before speaking. The look is not without some hypnotic fixation, rather like the stare of an old tom-cat directed towards someone it has doubts about. I search in my mind for some kind of remark to make so as to keep things going, something about the world being in such a terrible state, but the best I can muster is a look of sheepish agreement, and from the look he gives me back and the way he puts down the mug after taking a second drink of tea and takes up his newspaper again, without continuing with the subject, I can see he doesn't think much of my reaction. The silence thickens between himself and myself; my mother keeps working away, and I look across and see her falter in her movements, she becomes motionless in her kneeling position and seems to be gazing into the quiet glow of the low coal-fire. This is a habit she has, of suddenly pausing over any task, looking as though some memory has come to her, and then her lips start moving in prayer: 'Eternal rest give unto him, O Lord,' she whispers. (Who was she praying for—the little infant, the first-born, the child which my sister May told me she once saw the name of written in the big Book of Saints kept upstairs, locked away in the trunk, the child whose existence has never been mentioned to us?—or is it someone she knew, some young man perhaps that she met before she knew my father?) I see my father is about to speak, but he holds back, abrupt of speech though he is, for he will not interrupt such a moment. Yes, even he has the occasional awareness of a mood in another. The next thing, Mother is getting on with the polishing.

'I think,' says my father, 'I'd be as well put on the new mantle before the dark is in it.' 'Oh surely, surely,' agrees Mother, rising to her feet, 'if the mood is just on you. But do you know, I'd say there could be good life in the ould one yet.' 'There could,' says my father, 'an' there couldn't, woman, if that's not giving you a short answer.' From the way he stands up and the self-satisfied manner in which he puts the paper away I fancy he considers that something of a smart rejoinder.

This replacing of a gas mantle, I should point out, was no casual operation, fraught as it was with the risk of the mantle being damaged. The gas mantle was the cause of much annoyance and bickering in most homes, and in our own front kitchen gave rise to much exasperation in my father. A gas mantle, when removed from the box in which it was sold, was either cylindrical in shape—the upright model—or spherical—the inverted model, made of a stiffened cotton net; to be made ready for use, it had first to be deftly fitted in position on the fixture provided for it on the gas burner, then a lighted match had to be carefully applied to the lower edge, at which it would burst into a brief flame, burning away the stiffening additive, leaving a most fragile object to bear the brunt of daily use. It had the protection of a glass around it, but it needed only a heavy tread in the bedroom above, causing the ceiling to vibrate, to collapse a worn mantle. The naked light being used to light the gas mantle normally (a long taper in posh homes, a piece of folded newspaper lit from the fire in poor homes, and a match in the average home) needed to be held at the open top of the glass globe, and the timing in relation to turning on the gas had to be balanced: if put there too soon there would be a *pop* because the mixture was too weak, if delayed there would be a louder *pop* because it was too rich. Either of such could weaken a mantle, as could any less than delicate handling of the gas bracket. Few things were more irritating during the evening than gaslight which fluctuated, accompanied by hissing sounds. Only the best homes could afford to have a spare mantle at one side for emergency, so the average housewife, being mostly spent up by Wednesday, was in a state of regular emergency. The idea that a spare mantle, costing as much as tenpence, was lying in a drawer, 'doing nothing', as the phrase went, would have been ironic and intolerable when there wasn't a penny in the home for the gas meter.

'God curse the cross-eyed flamer who made that bloody gas mantle,' my father would suddenly call out, in a sort of suppressed roar, 'an' the hill and dale bloody rogues an' robbers down at the gas place—thinnin' the bloody gas with water.' (Water gas was used to dilute the coal gas—often in excess.) My mother would bless herself and make some whisper supposed to exorcize the curse in some way. (She had a way of quietly countering various aims of my father's which she considered unfitting. There was a neighbour named Dave, for instance, a most agreeable rascal he was, who almost never worked, had a most gentle-spoken wife from Cumberland, with brown eyes and a pale, lovely face, and five angelic small daughters; they were a most loving family, but seldom was there money to buy coal, and Dave was in the habit of creeping quietly along the backstreet after midnight with a bucket and stopping at our back gate. As my father was a miner, we got our coal by the load at much reduced cost, and we were the only family who kept it in a coal-shed in the backyard. The neighbours bought one or two bags a week and stored it in the back kitchen under the stairs. Dave would first put a finger through the latch-hole to see if the gate was barred, which was seldom. If it was, he would nimbly climb over, then open the coal-shed door and quietly fill his bucket, fasten the door and gate, and go off. My father noticed the coal stocks going down rapidly and suspected what was happening (Mother of course knew) and decided to put a stop to the pilfering by fixing a lock on the coal-shed door—a most unIrish thing to do. Mother made little comment, but every night she would see to it that the back gate was left open, the coal-shed door unlocked, and she would actually select a few handy cobs of coal and place them just inside the door to make Dave's filling of the bucket simpler.)

Mother winks for me to follow her into the kitchen—there is this continual sense of a conspiracy going on behind my father's back. I'll bet she's forgotten to buy the Christmas gas mantle, I think to myself. There would have been a number of mantles bought over the year, but no matter the state of the mantle my father always put a new one on for the festive evening, and the quality of the light it gave off would be good for ten minutes' worth of comment. I feel enough time has passed to allow me to go into the kitchen without it seeming obvious to my father that Mother and I are up to something.

'Do you think would you slip off to Denton's for me,' whispers Mother, 'and bring home a new gas mantle?' I'm inclined to be awkward but I spot the look in her face, the sweat, and the odd smut of soot. 'I'm ashamed of goin' into that shop again,' I say, 'I've been there seventy–nine times today already.' She gives me a hug to lead me out of the kitchen door. 'What present have you got me for Christmas?' I ask her. There is an uneasy absence of the feeling that presents are being put aside. 'Is it *presents* ye're asking, agraw?' she whispers in a mild, chiding way, 'sure wouldn't I give you the sun and moon, an' God forgive me, all the heavenly stars with them.' 'I know that, Mam,' I say, 'but it's not the same thing.' However, in spite of myself, I am somewhat mollified.

'A Veritas Incandescent Upright Gas Mantle, if you please, sir,' I tell Mr Denton at the corner-shop.

'Thawuntswut?' he says.

'The lad wants a gas mantle,' says Mrs Denton, 'don't you, love?'

'Yes, ma'am,' I say.

'Will you please shut up,' says Mr Denton to his wife. 'I know what he wants—I only want to hear him say it again—in the brogue. Ee, Willie—you're a rum lad, you are!'

I get back home with the gas mantle and find that my father has removed the tall glass cover and got rid of the old mantle, and mother is standing on the table entwining the long gas pendant that comes down from the ceiling with coloured paper in what seems to me a half-baked attempt to introduce some festive note.

'The light's goin',' says my father, 'the evenin' is in it.' The excitement is building up. 'I'll light a candle,' says my mother. She brings out one of the Irish brass candlesticks, puts a piece of candle in it, and, tearing off a thin strip of newspaper, gets a light for it from the fire.

'Willyeen, will ye take houlda the candlestick?' says my

father, 'An' see would you hould it straight at that—we don't want the place covered in grease.'

I look at my mother to see if she will help me escape—and she catches my look, for nearly all our intimate exchanges have to do with my desperate need to get out of my father's way, so that I can avoid being involved with him. Either she has much to do, or maybe she feels it won't do me any harm, so she puts on a bright ignoring of my plea. 'Here y'are, my fine son,' she says, thrusting the candlestick into my unwilling hand, and at the same time she looks me in the eye, and what she is saying is as though it were printed in words a foot tall: 'Take care now. Do nothing and say nothing that would upset that man your father, for you know how at a time like this the least thing will set him off.' I am inclined to give her a reassuring reply, but some spirit of devilment left in me makes me say with my eyes: 'What has it to do with me?' She catches my meaning and another look from her says: 'You'll see soon enough if you try any tricks!' And as if to give weight to her thought there is a shout from my father: 'Yerra take care with that flamin' ould candle—or you'll have me set on fire.' 'Arra what harm,' remarks my mother on the side, humming away as she polishes the dresser.

My father seems to have been in training all day for this task. He has taken no drink—maybe a humble pint but no more (perhaps he is wisely holding back for the evening, since he is not a man who can easily handle two bouts of drinking in the one day)—and is in that cool, calm mood that is seen on him in the evening, when he sits, pale and sober, waiting for the time he must go off to work—not unlike, I imagine, a man who might be going to the scaffold. This is almost too much for me, that sane look, the one of a man at peace with himself, for it sits so unnaturally on him that it makes me nervous, wondering when the outburst of temper will occur. I find myself holding the candle and him standing on a chair preparing to put the new gas mantle on, which he is now withdrawing from the box. If I were to go out in the street, stop any twelve–year–old half–timer from the cotton mill, and ask him to come in and put that mantle on, he would do it in half a minute. In fact Mother herself is quite a dab hand at it, having put a number of mantles on surrep-titiously when they have been broken during my father's absence at work. But she daren't mention this, and in any case it

164

seems that it is a ritual which must be performed by him alone on Christmas Eve.

He grips the new mantle right at the top, for there is a sort of conical head, where the fabric is bound together, with a firm bit protruding by which it is to be grasped. He now raises the mantle in his shaky hand and attempts to lower it over the upright pencil-like holder. This is a tense moment, but being blessed by some unusual deftness he puts the mantle on perfectly. Even the walls of the house seem to sigh with relief. To me it is a mild anticlimax. 'Well!' he won't say more than that, for he's not a man to push his luck. 'Hand me up the candle, Willyeen, and I'll burn it.' I hand him the candlestick. Already the evening darkening gloom has descended. My father, now somewhat relaxed and confident following his success with putting on the mantle, takes the candlestick from me in an assured manner. I have a sense of misgiving about this, assurance being alien to his nature, for there is something almost catlike about the way he normally hesitates over every move he makes. But for a moment he drops his nervous guard, and thrusts the candle toward the flame. There is a bright burst of flame, which dies down rapidly. Now my father turns on the gas tap, holds the candle near, and, like magic, the gaslight buzzes on. Hurrah! Thank God all is well! . . . steady on, is it? There is an odd silence about the place, as though voices are being held under. Then I spot a small, gaping wound in the side of the mantle, where the gaslight escapes the fabric and protrudes like a pale, uneasy bubble. 'He musta bloody punctured it wi' t'candle wick! I bloody knew he would!' A peculiar voice escapes from my father as his top teeth clasp down on his lower lip, reaching almost to his chin. 'May the divil shoot, roast, an' melt the flamer who first thought of that flamin' contraption,' I hear him hiss. Mother looks at me. She need not speak. I'm off to Denton's for a Veritas Incandescent Gas Mantle, Upright.

'Thawuntswut?' asks Mr Denton.

It seems to me that all this cannot be real, but is some awful nightmare that looks like lasting all my life. My thoughts turn to Adam and Eve, and I ponder over their rashness in misbehaving back there in the Garden of Eden—eating the forbidden fruit did not seem the whole story to me, but was just about plausible—and I thought not only had they got themselves turned out of what must have been a grand place to live, but on top of that they had made the whole of life so difficult for us millions following after. If only somone had told them properly! Ah well, some day one will be away from all the din and into the quiet grave. I wander back home through the streets, lonelier than any cloud. I get back in home and now it is dark, and a more risky procedure to mank about with the gas mantle by candle-light. I imagine that my father must have been saying in his heart, 'To hell with this home and the mantle, and the wife and kids too, come to that—I wish I were back in old Ireland, where there was no coal-mine, no streets and no noise—only the glow of the turf-fire in the little back room, and my cronies sitting round drinking their porter, and never a cross word—or very seldom—and the quiet comfortable evening before me.'

The gas mantle is finally put in place and the gas lighted. (I cannot bear the tension of a further telling.) There is a hammering on the front door, and a postman and his helpers are there—unable to decipher the name on two big parcels from Ireland: 'If they're Irish, sir, they're ours,' calls Mother. And she slips the postman a lavish Christmas tip. 'Oh, ta, missis—ta very much!' And he even touches his peaked cap. Oh, and now the wonderful excitement of opening the two badly-tied parcels—and inside each is a huge goose. Each fowl is praised —then my father feels at the breast and backside, and he tears away some sewing and out slides a big bottle of John Jameson whiskey. 'Michael Foudy,' he says, taking a handerchief from his pocket and dabbing his eye. 'Sure I told you they'd never forget us. God love you, Michael!' And after the swift tear he says: 'I think I'll drink their health—as early as it is.' 'Arra why wouldn't you,' says Mother, producing another bottle of whis-key from the inside of the other goose, which is from her sister Maggie. So my father takes the Foudy's whiskey, searches for the corkscrew in the table drawer, and engages in the antici-patory act of drawing the cork, a task more to his liking than fixing a new gas mantle. After drawing the cork and giving a delicate sniff at the whiskey-touched air he gets himself a clean, polished glass, and carefully pours himself a good tosheen from the bottle. I watch but know better than to speak, for this is is a moment he prefers to savour in his own form of silence, made up of low humming sounds coming from deep within himself, almost like a cat purring. He raises the glass to the light, and surveys the pale gentle fluid reverentially, murmuring at the

166

same time a blessing on the Foudy family, and now he downs it in the Irish fashion, at one, swift, gulp. 'Musha that's a great whiskey—a powerful whiskey altogether,' he remarks, in a voice touched with awe. 'That fellow would never think to ask had one a tongue in one's head,' I think to myself. Oh, the difference between him and Uncle William—and the gracious way Uncle would always give me a sip before himself.

My father now discovers something hidden down inside the parcel from Ireland—it is some kind of dark weed, like a leaf of some kind of seaweed. 'Look', he exclaims, 'look what they thought to put in—*duileasc*!' He takes the green weed and puts it into his mouth and begins to chew it, and to wail with the pleasure after a minute or two: 'Oh God save us,' he says, 'but that's a great thing—*duileasc*!' And so I take a piece of this and begin to chew it. First it is tough and tasteless, and then some deep salty tang comes out of it. 'I suppose it is great,' I say to myself, 'but one of the Irish things I've lost understanding of.' Just the same, I am not untouched by the sound of the Irish word—in a way no English word could get at me. And when I look at my father, and see the strange emotions alive in his face, I sense that feeling of special loss that must occasionally touch every immigrant, no matter what his race, colour, or creed, and despite all the security he may have earned in his new home, which hints at some deep-denied longing he has, to be his true self, to be in his own place in his own land amongst his own people. Not that I could realize I would inherit much of the same feeling, and that it would be there with me for the rest of my life.

'Musha I think maybe I'd go up to bed an' rest for half an hour,' he says. The emotion of everything is a bit too much for the old boy. 'Arra, why wouldn't you?' says Mother. 'What is there to stop you?' It is at such moments I sense the special tender understanding between them. He carefully builds up the fire so that it'll be burning fully in an hour or so. 'Take care would any of ye lay a hand on that,' he warns. Then he puts the two bottles of whiskey into the press, as he calls the triangular cupboard on the wall, and he goes upstairs praising aloud his friends back home in Ballyhaunis, as his footsteps sound on the bare boards.

With himself out of the way, Mother dances round the house, finishing off the last polishing jobs, and now the place is shining. And after that, she disappears into the back kitchen, closing the middle door. I sit by the fire that has the lively tongues of flame licking outwards and upwards. There is young James, I need to keep an eye on, my sister May has turned up, and Edward is now back. I'm thinking what an awful, depressing time Christmas is, creeping along on one. When I go into the back kitchen there is Mother almost ready. She is wearing a new blouse, and her hair is brushed and combed, glossy and wavy, and looks darker than it did before, and there is a nice velvet band around her neck with a gold locket attached to it, inside of which I know there is a curl of hair. She is wearing her best skirt and pretty black shoes, and there is an eager glow on her face.

'Mother,' I say, 'you look awful!'

'Do I now indeed,' she remarks.

'You look worse than awful,' I say, 'you look rotten.'

She has a tiny spot of red in each cheek—she must have put them on—and the effect is to make her look very attractive.

'Why wouldn't I,' she says, 'for sure amn't I only an ould oinseach.'

'You look worse than rotten,' I say. 'You look—'

She stoops and kisses me. There is a smell of some kind of scent from her. It really is wonderful. But the fact is, she seems to be really good-looking, and she is like some really nice-looking woman you might see out somewhere—and not so much like my dear old Mum going round the house, and this makes me uneasy. I don't like Mother not looking exactly like her ordinary self.

'It's all right,' I complain, 'everybody getting ready—but what have I to get ready into?'

'We'll see,' she says, and she goes down to a drawer in the back kitchen chest of drawers and takes out a paper parcel and brings out a new jersey. 'Let's see how it is for a fit.'

I take the jersey. It isn't exactly the jersey I would have bought, although it is a nice grey with a collar. But it hasn't got the pearl buttons I like to see. Still, it's a new jersey.

'Would it be all right if I had a wash,' I say, 'a good wash? Eh, Mam?'

Mother looks at the slopstone all clean and scoured, and the floor below it mopped and stoned, and the new roller-towel hanging on the door, and although she knows I'll make an awful mess of everything, she speaks in her warm, generous way. 'Wash away,' she says, 'wash as much as you like.' She is careful to avoid any warnings or criticisms, for she knows I don't like such, and they might, as she often remarks, take the good out of a thing. She looks for some old newspapers, and then she spreads them out on the floor. I unfasten my shirt-sleeves and whip off my old jersey and shirt at one go, getting a whiff of the old, weary sweat from under my arms, which will soon be washed away. The air to my skin seems to revive me in some way, and I stick out my chest and try to see it in the little looking-glass that hangs over the slopstone. 'And here's a new towel from the drawer,' says Mother. I take the towel and give her a kiss: 'You look grand, Mam,' I tell her. 'You do, honest.' In spite of myself, I feel the Christmas thing is getting a hold on me. But all the same, I cannot get away from a feeling that underneath all the fuss and merry-making, Christmas is a sad time. The odd thing is that no Christmas comes in the next sixty years without a sense of that same lonely, sad, and unfulfilled feeling. After all, wasn't it a sorry end in store for that babe in the manger—or so it must have seemed for the Holy Mother?

Uncle William is the first to arrive on Christmas Eve. Although it is dark, with the rolled-paper blind pulled down, I have managed to spot his coming, and the call is given to Mother, the door opened before him, and he gets his great welcome, so important a thing in our home. Uncle looks round the house, which is even brighter than on Saturday evenings, everything, from the huge, iron cauldron gleaming in the recess beside the fire, to the decorated gas chandelier, manifesting that spirit by which woman can bring something effulgent and welcoming to the poorest home. Uncle makes his shy smile, as though the magnificence of the place has quite staggered him, but reserves some surprise to turn on to Mother, for how pleasing she looks. The feelings are kept under control and played down, for one must never be so rash as to ignore those unseen presences which keep an eye on us. Mother's manner is changed, totally different from the one my father brings out in her, for Uncle inspires her with something of the Flemings, the family spirit, something lively and warm. In the light, happy laughter, the brightness of her eyes, and even the more upright graciousness of her bearing, there is a glimpse of what she might have been like before she met my father. It seems a sad thing in this life that so many of us are denied the kind of company and talk that bring the best out of us.

Uncle William recovers, dips into a pocket and takes out a bottle of Irish whiskey and puts it on the table. Mother gives a cry of thanks—although she wouldn't care if she never saw a drop of whiskey except when she has a windy pain. And the next thing he takes another bottle from some inner pocket, and now there are the two fine bottles of whiskey on the table. Next he has a present for young James, and he has a half-crown each for us others—a generous present indeed. But the main thing is the presence of Uncle William, for this changes the whole atmosphere, so that it becomes infused with a new and more happy spirit.

The door is opened again and in come Patrick and John Kirrane. There is something so powerful about Patrick, not merely in his broad-shouldered appearance and unsmiling face, but the impression he gives of strong feelings under the surface, that the room appears smaller when he enters. John, gentle and smiling, making his quiet, warm greetings after Patrick. *Thud, thud*—down on the table a bottle of whiskey from Patrick, and another one from John. In through the middle door comes Willie, who has been getting ready; he greets everyone and shyly, as though ashamed, produces a bottle of whiskey and awkwardly puts it down on the table. It seems there is something familiar about that bottle—but I keep my mouth shut, surely it is one of the bottles out of the geese from Ireland! Mother must have slipped it under her apron, taken it into the kitchen, and thrust into Willie's hand, for she wouldn't have him wasting his money on drink, nor would she have him feeling not up to the others.

The atmosphere is warming up, but there is no drinking just yet. My father comes in, and after giving his loud, awkward welcomes to everyone, he lets out grunts of pleasure and thanks at the sight of all the bottles of whiskey on the table. By gum, I'm thinking to myself, we must be a rich family. I'll bet there's not a house in the neighbourhood can brag of that much whiskey on the table on Christmas Eve. Father now brings out the whiskey from the Foudys, for he's going to let these Micks from the country see that he has influential friends in the town—and is not just the shopboy they take him for. The trouble with him—apart from his animosity—is the intensity with which he expresses everything he feels; there is no lightness of touch, rarely a waggish remark, but a fierce seriousness, except when he raises the special bottle of Jameson, to read the label, and then his manner is solemn, and his voice sinks into a pious hoarseness: 'Three star, seven year old!'

Mother has quietly moved the bottles out of the way and put them into the press, for she does not care for this display of drink, and now she spreads the huge, gleaming white tablecloth over the other cloth and this adds to the brightness of the place. There is this feeling of things going almost too well, one which Mother always plays down, perhaps feeling that it could get out of hand; she is apprehensive of excited enthusiasm, and also she may hope, with the bottles out of sight, to hold back the actual drinking until she would have food on the table, but if so my father defeats her in this. He has a bottle out and begins to pour and hand out the drinks—no water added amongst the Irish—and now Uncle gives me a wink to go across and join him for a first taste. The glass is up at my lips, and I do not mind that hot, blinding scurry of the whiskey as it runs down inside me, for I believe whiskey does me good, and I have learnt to toss it back pretty fast. 'I'll bet none of my mates in this street ever tasted whiskey,' I think to myself. 'What a lucky lad am I!'

This Irish drinking on such an occasion is never frivolous or boisterous, but animated by some ancient sense of ceremony, perhaps hinting at memories of greater days and nobler circumstances. And it would seem to me, as young as I am, so different are our Irish ways from those of Lancashire folk, that we each belong to quite separate worlds. We Irish are never without some word about God, the Holy Ghost and the Blessed Virgin, and we go whispering prayers and blessing ourselves a dozen times a day, often furtively—although all this does not preclude outbursts of temper and oaths: possibly allows for them—whilst those decent English people go along without seeming to give Him a thought, except perhaps on Sundays when they avoid whistling. Yet they appear to live more ordered and proper lives than any of us, and, whilst we take on some show of being Catholic, it is clear that their way of life is more estimable, the conscientious manner they go about their work, their absolute reliability and the uncomplaining manner, and above all, their marked sobriety and eschewing of violence.

Amongst us Irish, I often heard it said that we could learn a lesson in respectable living from them. Death too, which constantly comes into our talk—one speaks of the dead as though in some way they are still alive—is hardly mentioned by the good folk in our street. They, alas, appear to have forgotten the right way of behaviour at a funeral, and are uneasy and uncertain over expressing grief, although a most feeling people. Sleep was a sacred phenomenon to the Irish, one interrupted only in an emergency, but in Lancashire a woman would waken up her husband as he dozed in the rocking-chair after his day's work and ask him had he a penny for two ha'pennies for the gas meter, or one of the children might waken him and ask him was the clock right or was it fast, and he would supply the penny or the answer without any show of irritation and drop off to sleep again.

Meanwhile Patrick has put out feelers over the Christmas Eve tradition of sending the big cheque home to Ireland. There is a weekly custom observed by Patrick, when every Saturday he asks Willie: 'Did you write home?' There was the understanding at the time with regard to any Mayo single young man over in England that he send a weekly sum home, ranging from one pound downwards. That was the custom and commonly accepted, but few young men could live up to it. One pound was one-third of a miner's weekly wages, and as the young man had to pay for his keep and buy his clothes, and enjoy his drink, it put a tight rein on him. Patrick had now taken on a much harder job in the mine, doing piece-work on the coal-face, and could earn almost twice as much as a dataller, who was paid a fixed daily wage. Every week he would take a pound from his young brother John, and send it, along with his own pound, home to their mother, Aunt Maggie, my mother's eldest sister. To Patrick, the eldest son, this might appear as an investment, for, the father being deceased, he could take over the homestead whenever he chose to get married. Willie, who lived with us, paid one pound for his weekly board, had bought himself a suit or two on weekly payments, and found it difficult to keep going.

Patrick is set on sending not less than a twenty–pound Christmas cheque home—and it must be done before eight o'clock, at which time the post office closes. Like a gambler he puts down ten pounds on the table, and asks for Willie and John to make it into the twenty. But Willie and John have not ten pounds between them; the most Willie can rustle up is two pounds, and

John three. Patrick is annoyed and it is plain to see it in his manner. Uncle William shows that he does not like to see this sort of behaviour—Patrick pressing his brother Willie for money—nor does my mother care for it at all. There'd be no luck in any cheque there was variance over, for with her and Uncle things must be done with a dignified graciousness. Money itself is nothing, it is the good spirit that goes with it which really matters. There are a few uncomfortable moments, whispering between Willie and Mother in the kitchen, then Father is drawn in, and the money is found for Willie—a sort of loan as it were, all to pacify Patrick. He now asks John to go along with him to the post office to confirm that the money has been sent, but John will not even consider going, certainly not in that capacity. Patrick, not to be outdone, takes me along as a witness that he hasn't pocketed the money. He is a powerful man surely, and one feels it if only walking alongside him. And a pleasant enough fellow he is once he's out of the house and the money in his pocket. He walks with a swing—almost a fighting walk, and I'm glad there are no groups of young men at any street-corner, although it would be the rare one who would make a match for Patrick. He takes me into the Derby Street post office and arranges with the man behind the counter that an order for twenty pounds will be paid to Margaret Kirrane at the Knock post office back home in County Mayo. Then out we come, and he hands me a shilling, which I refuse, but which he presses on me, and I accept. It's not going to be too bad of a Christmas after all, the way things are going. Money in the pocket never fails to bring some uplift to me.

We get back home to find that Mother has the table laid and all the food out ready for everyone to sit and eat. It is what the Irish call a fast day—in fact a day of abstinence—and no meat is to be eaten the day before Christmas, so the main item is John West salmon, with large piles of bread and butter, a jug full of celery, then jam and cakes and other things, lashings of hot, strong tea, and of course a glass of whiskey set at every place. 'If that's a ghost,' remarks my father, as he raises and surveys the glass of whiskey, 'may it appear often.' He will repeat this in the manner of those men who prefer the sound of the same words in their voice to fresh words in the voice of another. Between whiskey and tea, and the nice, fresh bread and butter, with the salmon and other things, nobody could be said to be left hungry or wanting. Perhaps the main thing the men enjoy is my mother's tea, for she is a great tea-maker, using the best tea and plenty of it, and she is always up and down, brewing fresh pots. My father doesn't want us children to be at the table, but Mother and Uncle insist that we all eat at the one time.

I cannot recall any domestic scene since that day—and I have sat down to solid silver plates with friends, illustrious, or almost, and the best tableware that money could buy—to compare with the spirit of festive warmth in our little home in Bolton, the big coal-fire burning red and bright, the black, gleaming range, the new mantle purring and brilliant above us, the white tablecloth, scarcely seen for all the dishes that are on the table, the glugging sound from the whiskey as my father pours from a newly opened bottle, and above all, those handsome faces of the Kirranes and the smiling one of Uncle William. Even my father doesn't look too bad, and the gentle presiding beauty of Mother. Somehow all the eyes seem to be shining and the voices touched with laughter—but quiet gentle laughter, of course, for only an eejit would allow himself a burst of loud laughter that would draw attention to himself. Any ostentatious merry-making is considered unseemly, for all happy events are gifts from God, and should be celebrated with a quiet sense of thanksgiving. The beaming happiness itself is held under, for these men of the land will not be drawn into any exhibition of loud jollification by my father at the Christmas Eve table, since the famines are only a generation or two behind them, and more than a trace of the memory remains. As for the talk, it is always on the same almost wistful note: 'I wonder what they'll be doing at home at this hour: Will Ellen have gone up to your house I wonder?' Yes, it is all of Ireland.

When the meal was over and the things cleared away, Father insisted on my brother Edward playing the fiddle. There were three tunes from Ellwood's First Tutor Book for the Violin: *The Blue Bells of Scotland*, *The Minstrel Boy*, and *The Last Rose of Summer*, and any one of the three, played on the thirty–shilling fiddle, by a boy who had been learning only a short time, could bring tears to his eyes. Father was inclined to sing, but Uncle William sternly hushed him, as fond as he himself was of a song: 'We are in a strange land,' he said reprovingly, 'amongst a people who have lost their men out at the war, and others not home yet. I would walk out of the house this minute rather than

I hurt any one of these decent people, for surely this is not a time or a place for singing.' 'Sure you're right, William,' said my father, 'no matter where you go you must never go agin' the custom of the country.' He went on, 'never go agin' that wherever you go.' He looked at me as one giving a child sound advice. This would be only one of the many occasions in which there might be a threat of sharp words springing up between Uncle William and Father with regard to England and the English in relation to the Irish. But an actual encounter never took place, for my father was always quick to withdraw or smooth things over. Uncle William had an abhorrence of violence, combined with a great faith in the English, above all the English upper class and the English government (of which institution my father considered every man jack to be a rogue and blackguard). Uncle appeared to believe that the English had tried to do right by Ireland, that Ireland was better being under the English, and—as I recall hearing him say—that, given time, the English would always do the decent thing. 'Where would Ireland be but for the English?' he would ask. There was, as I may have indicated, some deep sense of appreciation in my Uncle William of the English character, of the reliability of the English word when given, of the orderliness and regularity of English life generally, that suggested he found all this more congenial to him in the rounds of daily life than he did the Irish ways. But when it came to the spontaneous need of the heart and spirit to rejoice, the Irish were needed.

My father had affection for his English work-mates and pub friends, but saw the real English as powerful right-wing politicians, judges, mine-owners, and the like. His Irish patriotism was perhaps his one true sentiment. I recall an occasion which I feel to be one of those intense moments of childhood—where the real meaning only comes years later, but which even at the time hints at things of deep importance. It was in the aftermath of the war prosperity, there were terrible troubles in Ireland, and I was up near Daubhill Station one afternoon, and amongst the rush of black-faced anonymous miners I saw one odd lonely figure, walking by himself, seemingly in thought: 'Hello, Dad' I said. He looked at me for a moment and said: 'Willyeen!' Then, revealing the one thought that was on his mind, and which set him apart from the others, he whispered to me: 'Tell me, is he still alive—MacSwiney?'

It is more than likely as the Christmas evening goes on that Paddy Conboy will look in to pass the season's compliments —and sure enough he does. Dear Paddy, what a wonderful visitor he is to our home, with his round, cheerful face, quick, blue eyes, and the wide moustache. Paddy was a navvy for Gornalls, and it was a job that seemed to sit most graciously upon the man, for it was good to see him when he would be going to or coming from work, in his bellbottom corduroys, with the leather yorks strapped just below the knee, the stout claubered boots, the good flannel shirt across his broad chest, and the coloured silk handkerchief round his neck, fastened neatly at the throat, with the loose, open jacket, and the tuft of curls showing below his cap. For three months of the year he might be drinking rather heavily and the other nine months he'd have the pledge. Paddy would walk often through Deane Clough on his way to work, and more than once, when it chanced to be a fine morning and he heard the birds singing, he'd turn back home, put on fresh clothes, for he had plenty, stick a couple of handkerchiefs and an extra collar into his pocket—he wouldn't be seen carrying a bag—and off home he would go to Ireland, taking the first train and the first boat.

Paddy is the greatest friend of Mother and Uncle William, from their part of the country, and with Paddy present my father cannot break up the talk, for he is a powerful talker, and remembers every incident and person from childhood—and he goes on from then to talk of life and death: 'D'you know, Maria,' he says, addressing himself to my mother, 'I don't mind dying at all—indeed I look happily to it—*if only all my dear friends will die at the same time with me.*' Paddy brings out his handkerchief, for he doesn't know whether he is going to laugh or cry, and it seems he does a bit of both. 'Sure death itself, God save us, won't it come to each one of us but I cannot bear to think that all the ones I love will be left in the world, drinkin', talkin', an' singin'—an' myself put down stiff and lifeless into the cold grave.' And so vivid is this thought with Paddy that it brings on a sort of melancholy which my mother has to cheer him out of: 'Wouldn't it be worse an' far worse, Paddy,' she says, 'if all your friends were to go first an' you left behind?' 'Shtop! shtop, Maria!' cries Paddy, 'but wouldn't that be death altogether—to be left behind.' And some thirty years or so later, when poor Paddy was actually dying, in Townley's Hospital, Bolton, he looked up at the faces beside the bed and asked: 'Who will drive me?' 'But to where?' they asked. 'To Holyhead surely,' he said, 'for the Irish boat—'.

(The thought has come to me that with the civilized peasant, as with the true poet and his like, the talk is nearly always of people, of Johnny this, Paddy that, and Seamus or Maggie the other, and what can you do with people only love, talk, fight, or merry-make. Those who can talk sensibly about money and property, or about architecture and literature, or about a dozen other subjects, have the benefit of a sort of leavening to life—you don't need drink to talk on these subjects. But for talk of people a glass of whiskey or wine is a great help and this keeps their feet on earth, as it were; but the peasant and the poet must of necessity be in the air, most of the time—drinking, talking, maybe dancing, even fighting, but whatever it is, doing the thing that can only be done with and amongst people.)

My father wants to send me to bed, but backed by Uncle I won't go. Then Paddy has to go home to his wife Lizzie, a decent Bolton woman, who, between herself and her mother and sister, have Paddy spoilt with attention. Then, as the time draws near for Patrick and John Kirrane to be off, I see Patrick beckoning Willie out the back to have a word with him. The talk and chatting go on. Then I go into the kitchen to Mother. Suddenly the back kitchen door opens and in comes Willie. He has his handkerchief up to his mouth. It seems that Patrick has had words with him out in the backyard, struck Willie a blow, and gone off back to his lodgings by the back gate. Mother is shocked: 'Arra, how could he strike you,' cries Mother, 'that never said a wrong word to a soul in this life!'

Suddenly there seems to be an odd shift amongst the men, for now they are like children before Mother. 'I think it was over the cheque, Maria,' says Willie. 'The divil melt the cheque,' says Mother. 'How could he ever lay a hand on you—that was a disgraceful thing to do—if your mother over in Ireland was to hear of this she would never forgive him—she would never let him into the house—that he would do a thing like that, and on this holy Eve of Christmas—and I tell you all he will never set foot in this house until he puts that thing right—he will never sit at my table again—a man who could do that to his own brother —and to you, Willie, above all people.' And somehow everyone goes quiet, even my father, and a sudden sadness has fallen over our Christmas Eve celebration. Mother was right after all. It is always unwise for people to abandon themselves to merry-making, since it seems to have a way of coming to a sorry end—and as she would often remind us, there was never luck where there was too much drink.

# 19

In the year of 1920 there was revealed to me on the streets and among the people of Bolton an English spirit I had but got glimpses of in industrial Lancashire. I had not known the town before the Great War, and had taken the rather grim atmosphere of those years as being the natural one of a serious and hard-working people, not at all inclined to gaiety like the Irish. But now that there was an end to the bloodshed, no more fear of a telegram being delivered to some family telling of a father or son lost in action, and now that, also, the terrible flu epidemic had finally disappeared, there was a sudden resurgence of what I had never imagined—the essentially happy and cheerful nature of the English. I could hardly believe it, and the merry sights so surprised and gladdened me that I found I loved the people and the place.

It all began just before May Day, when there were May Queen processions around the streets, in which small groups of girls dressed up in old borrowed clothes and shoes, paraded behind and about their selected queen, long trailings of old curtains tailing behind. These May Queen groups were quite charming at first, but it seemed that the girls couldn't stop parading, and they were prolonged almost to June, until they became dull affairs, except when arguments or fights broke out amongst the girls as to who should be queen. The most exciting pageantry was put on by boys as Maypole Dancers. From our street, and indeed from almost every street nearby—except the posh ones —gangs of lads abruptly turned from arguing, fighting, kicking tin-cans around, playing pitch-and-toss and telling tales, to having their Maypole Dance. It was an unbelievable switch, and one of such novelty that it took me some time to accustom myself to it. I began to understand why the season of spring—hardly getting a mention among the Irish—was so celebrated in poetry, song, and dance among the English. It seemed to start off almost spontaneously—someone had spotted maypole preparations in a street up Daubhill, where Charlie

Unsworth, a Labour candidate, had a fruit shop. Arguments and disagreements would break out at once, for street-corner boys do not readily agree with each other—agreement being considered a form of weakness—until finally it was realized that it was the first of May and time to dance. Everyone started moving then; one lad would rush home and come out with a long broom-handle, another would better this with a pole, on the top of either of which would be nailed a wheel from an old baby-carriage, in such a way that it would revolve freely, and to this wheel would be attached numerous long cords or lengths of thick banding. Infectious excitement would spread, and the lads would scurry into their homes in search of old clothes in which to dress up. Because of the ready availability of old skirts and shawls most of them would turn up dressed as old women, wearing bonnets, their faces often blackened with soot; others might be dressed as girls, with their faces chalked over. There were boys of a more artistic bent from nearby streets who on big occasions insisted on appearing as real girls—female impersonators of a sort—with their cheeks rouged, hair made up in a bob, and fastened with a ribbon. This sort of thing created embarrassment amongst our lot, the black-faced wenches, for the artistic ones really did look like girls, and took their roles seriously, but, in the way of boys out to have some fun and earn a few coppers, such incongruities were dissolved in the spirit of the thing. When the group had all gathered, and the arguments as to who should hold the pole and who dance had been settled, there was the more serious business of choosing the collectors. It was grand to have a bit of fun, but if you could make a few bob at the same time it gave the whole thing some meaning.

The bad eggs are sorted out and reliable collectors are agreed upon, and also a stout lad for the pole-carrier. The group leaves the street-corner, having decided on the route and the most likely stopping spots for the dancing, and it is expected of the boy holding the pole to keep a sharp eye on the collectors. Discord would often break out before the first dancing spot was reached, for these lads, having shed their normal clothes—the clothes were restrictive, the heavy clogs, thick braces and the like—would start scampering around, laughing and dancing, swinging their skirts in the air, letting out falsetto whoops, and giving chorus-girl kicks, causing the lengths of rope or cord which hung from the wheel to become entwined, or shoes to fly in the air. In getting rid of their clothes and donning a comic female costume there was a distinct change of personality, and normally sober boys would get up to the oddest capers. But since there was no shortage of the serious-minded Lancashire type, those that became over-exuberant would be brought to heel.

It was a jolly sight, and to me a moving one, to see all my mates set up their maypole at the nearest corner and suddenly start dancing. I could hardly believe the sight—it was as though some vital human impulse, denied expression for the rest of the year, had suddenly burst into life. With all the neighbours gathered watching, and the unexpected singing and skirling, the scene became so animated that it seemed the corner gaslamp and all the little houses might join in, and the entire street start dancing. I would feel myself struck by a swift, strange joy at the sigh of all my mates cavorting, skirts swirling, eyes shining, and their usually rough voices now rising sweet and clear above the confines of the narrow street. *Dancing round the Maypole,* they sang, *merrily we go!* These must be the real English, I thought, so unlike the multitude that hurried back and forth between home and mill every day, with not a moment to spare. So it wasn't a fable. There must have been a Merrie England once before industry took over. Now they were doing a toe-dance and singing *Hip-a-pip-a-cherry!* Underneath they are just like us Irish, I reasoned, only they're better dancers and singers. I found myself full of a new love for them all and I longed to join them. But I dare not, for there was that hint of begging money from the passer-by about it, which the Irish of our sort must never engage in. Oh, but I was greatly drawn to them and the scene!

These maypole dances rather set off the spirit of summer—or at least those touches of it that we were to witness in Bolton, and since the seasons also happen within one's heart, our appreciation may have been as rich as anybody else's. And so, when June came, the street atmosphere—given a boost by the Daylight Saving Time, which had come in during the war—was just right. Around half–past six on warm, summer evenings the chairs would appear at almost every front door and window in the street, and girls begin to organize their games. Those young, girlish figures, whom one had scarcely glimpsed all the long, winter months suddenly appeared, singing their melodious street songs as they played their games. And what was even stranger was the appearance of the little doffers and tenters from the card-room, brought from seclusion, it seemed, by the young voices in the streets. These were the girls, aged thirteen or fourteen, who a year or so before had been part of the ordinary, lively, schoolgirl element of the street-scene, often much more spirited than the boys, but now, after a few months in the card-room, they would age rapidly, the schoolgirl bloom and daintiness departing, and a white skin, mottled with black-heads and pimples, taking its place; with this went a curious change in temperament, a sort of shrinking from meeting people, as though feeling degraded in some way, and after the girls got home from work in the evening, the mothers would often complain that they could never get them to go out. 'Sits there she does, our Edna, starin' into t'fire, an' you daren't say a flamin' word to her, she bites your 'ead off. I don't know what's come over 'er sin' she started work—you can't speak to her. Most weekends she comes in that front door of a Sat'day dinner-time an' she never sets foot outside until Monday mornin' when she goes off t'mill again. It's not as though she'd no clothes—I got 'er a luv'ly coat at Christmas. It can't be good for the poor girl, but I don't know what to do! I mean you can't kick 'em out.'

Yet other girls might be affected in a different way by mill work, parading home in their mill dirt and clogs in groups of four or five, arms so firmly linked that they would knock you over rather than disengage, and at the same time they would bawl out tales to one another, make fun of anybody they saw, and, being secure in a group, would laugh and screech and indulge in vulgar repartee with boys. The retiring girls would be seen watching the games from behind the curtains at first, then would appear on the doorstep, and would finally be persuaded to make up a side at rounders, and in a few minutes the rigidly withdrawn personality would ease, then blossom, and before the evening was out the girl would be laughing, 'Ee, but I 'ave *enjoyed* myself!' she would exclaim, as though enjoyment was the last thing to expect in this life.

It was that same summer of 1920, when I was ten years old, that I fell in love with a girl called Alice. Alice lived in our street, and it would be easy to imagine some scruffy little girl, coming, as Alice did, from a two-up and two-down home like our own, set in amongst a maze of streets and cotton-mills, but this impression would be totally wrong. Alice was fairly tall and carried herself with a modest, erect pride; there was only an inch difference in our height, which I was pleased I had, but she was five days older than me, which irked me until I accepted that I could do nothing about it. She had a lovely head of hair, which during most of the summer she wore in long ringlets down her back, and at other times had it in two thick, glossy plaits. Her hair was silky to the touch, and this I knew intimately, for once when Alice and I were out alone in the country—having secretly escaped from our street—sitting on the grass near a brook, she warmly agreed to my impulsive suggestion that I be allowed to plait her hair. In those days the dressing of hair was a common family activity, and I had this sudden urge to handle Alice's lovely hair. The memory of that strange, silent excitement as I first combed, stroked and divided Alice's long tresses, preparatory to the actual plaiting, returns to me as I write, producing a curious tingle in the palms of my old hands. (When I first read, 'There is great mystery, Simone, in the forest of your hair,' many years later, the thought of Alice came back to me at once.) I began blithely enough with my unaccustomed task, after first getting my fingers used to the peculiar sensation of handling her rich long hair and the experience of looking closely at the nape of her pretty neck, and now and again seeing her smile as she made to turn, and listening to her talk and laughter. Suddenly this playful mood was interrupted by touching upon some strange and deep-down force: I found the control going from my fingers, the strength leaving me and a blurring of sensations, and I had to stop, to give up, make an excuse that I was making a mess of it, and get up and go off and pretend to look in the water to see if I could spot any fish. It took some long minutes for the peculiar mood to lift and allow me to return to my ordinary self.

She was once giving me a kiss when the breeze brought her silky tresses down between our faces, and it was such a lovely moment—to feel her hair caressing my forehead and eyelids. I have heard talk of women versed in the wiles of lovemaking, and indeed have not escaped encounters with an inamorata or two, but all their skills I fancy to be little compared to the magic of that moment when Alice's hair slipped down between our faces. I remember how I always thought of her hair as being *auburn*; Alice has *auburn* hair, I would say, when I was playing at describing her to myself. This word auburn was used of the hair of most heroines in those days, and I was fond of the word (attractive words, like so much else, were scarce around Bolton), and I couldn't bear for Alice's hair to be denied it. Once at home when the talk got round to hair—hair and eyes were much noted at the time—and after carefully remarking on the colour of the hair of other girls playing in the street, I casually mentioned Alice and her auburn hair, but my sister May turned on me: 'Giveover,' she said, 'it's not auburn—it's not a bit auburn—if you ask me, it's goin' on more for mouse colour.' I also recall a remark my mother made when she was looking out the window over the low curtain at a group of girls playing a street game: 'Look out at Alice there,' she said to my sister May, 'she seems to have awful long arms.' I looked first and saw my dear Alice standing on the sideset, and I had only to hear her name, let alone see her, to feel this peculiar quickening motion at my heart, and something funny happen in my throat. 'Long!' I said, 'they don't look long to me.' As a matter of fact, they did look rather long—now it was pointed out—but to me most attractively so. My sister May had to chirp in: 'They're nearly down to her knees,' she said. 'That's the proper length of arms, Mam,' I said—I wouldn't bother to argue with sister May. 'It's us,' I went on, 'have short arms. All of us. They'd hardly go down to a right person's elbow.' I gave a sly look at May and thought I'd be as well leave it at that.

Alice's forehead was broad and placid (I've learnt to be on the lookout for the woman with a narrow, restless forehead—they give no one any peace), her gentle blue eyes were large and wide-set, nose not small yet shapely, mouth full, and lips soft. She was an only child, came from a good home—Dad a corporation paviour, full-time work—wore a clean frock every day, and exuded a natural fragrance. I had known Alice for some years, of course, but never to talk to on her own. There was some innate disparity between boys and girls, aggravated by our way of life into hostility—tinged with a show of contempt by the male and mild disgust by the female. I got acquainted with Alice, however, by a fortunate chance. An infant called Abraham used to visit the Howarth family in our street; he was about two years old, not yet breeched, with a dirty face, soiled frock, and clogs with sharp irons on the bottom, and when he saw me he would run towards me and leap into my arms. I had never known it to happen to me before, and felt flattered that a child whom I had only casually met should take such a liking to me. One evening whilst I was holding Abraham, Alice came up: 'Billy,' she asked, 'would you like me to hold him?' (If anyone should imagine that in the interest of realism I am going to allow Alice to drop an aspirate I'm afraid they are mistaken.) The way she said 'Billy' sounded quite different from how I had ever heard it before, and made me feel a new person, just as though another Billy had been under the ordinary one, and Alice had somehow brought him to life.

'Eh—what?—oh, pardon—yes—' I stammered. 'Abraham,' I said, 'go to Alice.' And I held him out to her. Abraham didn't want to go to Alice but he may have gathered that it would please me if he went to her, and even at that age he must have been vaguely aware of beauty, and certainly he could not have surrendered himself to a more lovely young person than Alice. I handed him over, and she came close to me to take him. Our hands met, then our eyes exchanged a strange look, and, sensing what had to be the unspoken, they now looked down on the smudged face of Abraham. And as the weight of the boy Abraham passed from me to Alice, there was set going some pulse of love and longing in me, felt strangely between breast and throat. It was as though in that moment in that crowded, noisy street on a summer evening, Alice was to become part of my whole life—and considering it was all so long ago, and the feelings about it are so closely clear to me today, maybe I was not so far out. After all, it is surely in the heart alone that we possess anyone, for either good or bad.

Abraham played up to the scene, and there was a bit more handing over from Alice to me, and I to Alice, all of which I was not averse to, and some chasing around and the like. (Bless you, Abraham, lad, wherever you are this day.) The next thing, Alice was called off by the girls to join in some singing games, and Abraham's mother came for him, and for some minutes I went around the street, my heart high and dazed and full of love for humanity, when suddenly there broke through my dazed daydreaming a voice singing: 'B stands for Billy'o, bonny, bonny Billy'o . . .' I realized it was Alice's voice, and the next thing two girls grabbed me by the hands and pulled me into the circle. 'Cum on—don't be shy!' one said. 'Aye,' said the other, 'you're the chosen one!' And I heard Alice's voice, warm and proud it was, and so light and fresh: 'If I had a one to choose I'd choose my bonny Billy'o! . . .' The words went round in my head it seemed, and when her song came to an end I waited for the laugh to come with the chase, but there was no laugh. 'She means it,' I thought—'Ee, a girl loves me!' I almost choked with happiness. 'She's declaring our love to the whole world,' I thought. 'Ee, I'm in heaven! And thank God we're at the bottom of the street and my mates at the top corner can't see me.'

That summer of 1920 was one of the happiest of my life. (One is perhaps never quite as happy again, or at least not in the same innocent way, throughout puberty and adolescence, youth, early manhood, manhood, middle age, and old age, until extreme old age, when—or at least so I hope—there is a tranquil dying down and ultimate extinction of carnal desire; although I rather fear that when that goes, much else goes with it, including spiritual longing.) I soon discovered that the more cunning you are in attempts to conceal your love from the world, the more likely you are to let the hint slip out that will tell all. There was the street, thronged with young and old, yet from the moment I fell in love with Alice, it seemed there was no way of hiding it—no matter how often I told myself that it was hidden away in my heart, and no one but she could know. It was the strangest feeling, the way it came creeping up all over me causing me to be husky in my throat, so that I could hardly speak, making me happy and unhappy in turn, then congealing into a large lump round my heart. 'Crikey, I'm losing all control of my blooming self,' I thought 'what's come over me!' Mother turned to me one day. 'Tell me, agraw,' she said, 'you look strange—are your little bowels all right?'

There was no easy way of our meeting or getting in touch with each other, but soon I overcame my intense shyness, became reckless, and we arranged meetings well away from the street, and even went for walks and tram rides together. On one occasion going out to the country we arranged that Alice get on the Dunscar tram at one stop and I should get on at the next —but either I put my hand out too uncertainly or the tram driver didn't see me, for the next thing the tram went clanging by without me and with Alice seated downstairs.

I enjoyed kissing her, and she never refused me—I rather felt she ought now and again—and we both used to lean forward, hands behind our backs, when we kissed. One incident to do with Alice stays clear in my mind. There was an old lady known as Ma Clarkson, who kept a sweet shop, and was a friend of my mother's. In her own way Ma Clarkson was considered to be rather posh, she spoke well, had large teeth, all her own, a country complexion and she wore a paisley shawl, all unusual in our area. It was whispered in our home—I was there, eaves-dropping, when Ma Clarkson actually whispered it—that she had had one son, and there was an actual photograph of him in Ma Clarkson's little parlour, a handsome young man who had gone on the stage in London. It seemed an unbelievable dis-tance from the Bolton of those days to the London stage. Mrs Clarkson's son had made it, but had come to a sad end: 'Drugs,' was the word she whispered to my mother, and 'God rest his little souleen,' sighed Mother, as though talking of a baby and blessing herself as the same time.

On this certain day I arranged a rendezvous with Alice at the window of Ma Clarkson's shop, a spot which would attract no notice since looking into shop windows was a common occu-pation, even when one had no money. I got there first, with sixpence in my pocket and eager to show off. Alice turned up a few minutes later and we stood a yard apart, each gazing in the window. Then I saw that the street was quiet and I whispered, 'Come on, follow me.'

The shop door was always shut tight, and I had to force it open, whereupon a loud bell clanged; I held the door like the little gentleman I took myself to be, and ushered Alice in. It was a tiny shop, down a step to get inside, and almost like entering a magic cavern, so crammed was it with shelved full of jars of sweets—humbugs, mints, pear drops, butterscotch, and behind the counter, out of the reach of hands, trays of caramel toffee. The air seemed alive with delicious smells. The clang of the bell brought Ma Clarkson out of her cosy back room, and although I had intended to pretend that Alice and I weren't together I greeted her and introduced Alice. After all it counted as some-thing to let Alice see that I was on a personal footing with someone who owned a shop.

Now came the exciting moment of choosing the various sweets, for sixpence was a large sum and allowed for consider-able choice. There were rum-and-butter toffees, favourites of mine, and Roocroft's nut-milk cubes, and even Mackintosh's selection, although they were on the expensive side. I lightly suggested these to Alice, but smilingly she declined, and said that what she wanted were sweets known as *Names*. Ma Clarkson brought the box to the counter, flat, lozenge-shaped sweets, each one with a name on it, and underneath a special motto for the person who bore that name. It was hard to hide my disappointment, for it seemed to me that of all the sweets in the shop these must be the most childish ones, sweet and insipid, ranking with dolly mixtures. And when I asked Alice how much she wanted—hoping she would say 'Oh just a penn'orth,'— she said, 'I leave it to you.' Ma Clarkson took up her small brass scoop and began to delve lightly into the sweets and put them on the scale. 'Oh a few more, please,' I heard myself say.

Those sweets cost fourpence, and I bought her a pennyworth of caramel toffee to chew and some pear drops for myself. My high expectations had been so dashed that it was an effort to pull open the shop door and hold it for Alice as we stepped out into the street—my fine sixpence gone and so little in return.

'Oh darling,' cried Alice, picking out a sweet, 'I've got a *William*!' She must be a bit daft, I thought, to imagine I would take an interest in a few words dyed into a sweet. She read it and exclaimed: 'And it's exactly you!' I put on a bogus air of interest and at the same time thought, I wish I'd stayed at the street-corner with all my mates and my sixpence in my pocket. '*William*,' she read, '*Loved by all*.' 'What—what?' I said. '*Loved by all*!' she called, and looked round and kissed me.

Alice handed me the *William* sweet and I read it twice. I always knew there was something special about me, I thought, but never knew rightly what it was. The man who wrote those words knew a thing or two. It seemed that my low spirits picked up at once as I put the sweet carefully away in my pocket. I kept it for days, weeks, months, until it had shrunk and the words had faded away, but it remained a little talisman for me, and any time I felt depressed I would put my fingers into the pocket and feel the fragment of the sweet and murmur to myself: '*William: Loved by all*!'